KEITH TEMPLE

ACKNOWLEDGEMENTS
THE AUTHOR AND PUBLISHERS WOULD LIKE TO THANK THE FOLLOWING PEOPLE FOR THEIR GENEROUS ASSISTANCE IN THE
PREPARATION OF THIS BOOK:

ENGLAND
KEN BERRY (WIZARD ELECTRONIC GAMES), KEITH BEST, JEREMY BRENT, BICKS AUTOMATICS,
TONY CLARKE, ANDREW CROSS, PHILIP CROW, JEAN AND ALAN CROW, JAMES DALGETY
(PUZZLE COLLECTION), BRIAN DAVEY (NOSTALGIA AMUSEMENTS), PETER HEATH, GEOFF
HARVEY, TIM HUTLEY, STEPHEN MAY, JOHN OFFENBACH, TREVOR OWEN, THE PINBALL
OWNERS ASSOCIATION, MARTIN RUBY, SCORES LTD., BOB THOMSON, JOHN WILKINSON, JOHN ZOLD,

TWO RARE WOOD-RAILED PINTABLES FROM THE GOLDEN AGE — THE 1950S —
WILLIAMS' **CROSSWORD** AND GOTTLIEB'S **ROTO-POOL** ARTWORK BY GEORGE
MOLENTIN AND ROY PARKER RESPECTIVELY.

CONTENTS

FOREWORD

BY GORDON MORISON

ARTIST GORDON MORISON WITH HIS FRAMED PLAYFIELD ARTWORK FOR GOTTLIEB'S **SPIDERMAN**, JUST ONE OF THE MANY FROM HIS 20 YEARS IN PINBALL ART.

*I*t was a little disconcerting to be invited to write the foreword to this book. To an artist the paintbrush is mightier than the typewriter, particularly when you've got a typewriter like mine that can't even spell properly!

I started out around 1970 when I was under exclusive contract to one of the major pinball manufacturers, Gottlieb, at the Advertising Posters company in Chicago, thinking I was going to fill in for six months until another job came up. That six months ran into 20 years! I eventually became head of the art department at Ad. Posters which handled all the big pinball manufacturers at that time, and I did the artwork for hundreds of pinball machines. (The artist is responsible not only for the backglass graphics but the playfield, the plastic lightshields, and the cabinet.) And with two-player and four-player versions, and those for the Italian and German markets, I was so darned busy it was all I could do to keep my head above water. I didn't have any time to reflect on the history of pinball.

Pinball was then just a job. Now it's got a strong element of nostalgia. In fact to be honest we were a little ashamed of the work and were sorry we weren't working in advertising agencies. Moreover there were very few perks. When Kevin O'Connor recently worked on the Data East Playboy game he was invited to stay at the Playboy Mansion for a whole week. I remember when I worked on celebrity machines like *Charlie's Angels* I had to work from photographs and never even met them! I kind of hoped the girls would come and lay down in my office and let me trace round them, but they never did!

When I first started at Ad. Posters we were working in an area of Chicago that was so dangerous you could sometimes look out of the office window and see them firing at the police below from Cabrini Green just down the street. The area was going down at that time, and arsonists were continually setting buildings on fire so that some days it looked as though a war was being fought.

Pinball is a peculiar art but I do think its designs have an historical significance. In fact galleries are now selling pinball backglasses as works of art, and two years ago one big gallery in New York had an exhibition of them. I'm even collecting them myself — I've got closets full of the blessed things. Some day we're going to see all these machines — if there are any of them left — sitting in museums. It seemed to me we were turning out so many of the games we ought to be up to our armpits in them by now!

There were some awfully good artists working in pinball, there really were, and there still are. Some of these guys are supertalents. In the old days we didn't have the equipment they have now, such as Xerox machines and sophisticated photographic equipment. We didn't do any photographic work — all the silk-screen stencils were cut by hand, even the black outlines. Those guys cutting stencils could achieve incredible results. But things could also go badly wrong. One time an artist dropped a brush on the acetate for the artwork, and you know the mess that leaves behind. He did retouch it with white paint, but the separators work on the reverse side and he forgot about that. They flipped it over and faithfully reproduced every bit of mess that his brush had made as it rolled down the artwork!

Another memory from the old days is that you were never allowed to sign your work. I used to try and sneak it in somewhere but they'd make me take it out. Nowadays the whole of the design team get their credits on the machine, and it's pleasing to see these artists receiving the recognition they deserve. The modern pinball machine is a wonderful piece of technology with a lot of creativity behind it, but without the artwork where would it be? Those graphics have undergone many changes in the last 60 years, reflecting the changing tastes, attitudes, and technologies through the decades. There's a story here and I'm looking forward to going back through the years and exploring the history of the world of pinball art. I'm proud to have been a part of it.

Gordon Morison

*ALL THE ARTWORK FOR GOTTLIEB'S **SPIDERMAN** HAD TO BE APPROVED BY MARVEL COMICS BUT GORDON MORISON STILL MANAGED TO HIDE SEVERAL GIRLS' NAMES IN HIS BACKGLASS DESIGNS.*

HAPPY PINBALLERS AT PLAY IN THE BACKGROUND DETAIL OF GOTTLIEB'S 1964
BOWLING QUEEN. (ROY PARKER)

A PINBALLER'S PARADISE (1983). THIS ARCADE IN HOLLAND
FEATURES DOZENS OF PINBALL MACHINES, ALL MAINTAINED IN TOP
CONDITION.

INTRODUCTION

*S*everal years ago I wrote to BBC Television's *Nationwide* programme suggesting they might be interested in a feature on pinball. A few days later I had a telephone call from a producer: 'Tell me', he said in public school tones, 'what exactly *is* a pinball machine?'

There can surely be few people who have led as sheltered a life as this producer. Today pinball machines are everywhere. To begin with, though, they had a rather sleazy image — they were the preserve of the seedy tavern, run-down amusement arcade, and were perceived as the plaything of the backward! In more recent times they have become the accessory of trendy advertising agencies and the toys of the rich and famous: Elvis Presley, Steven Spielberg, Sammy Davis Jr, and *Playboy* founder Hugh Hefner have all been pinball addicts. It has even been said that Winston Churchill had one installed at his country home at Chequers during World War II. You can hardly envisage a better boost to wartime morale than playing a pintable carrying the name Victorious.

Researching this book was a fascinating exercise and brought me into contact with many interesting characters involved in pinball art. Perhaps Gordon Morison summed it up when he unearthed some of his dust-covered original artworks for me: 'Maybe your book is why I saved all this stuff.' I have also attempted to reveal some of the stories and anecdotes which lie behind many of these games and I hope I have done justice to all the excellent artists involved.

Pinball artwork has been a much admired but equally much neglected field to which many different artists have contributed over the years. Trying to unravel its history has been like piecing together a jigsaw puzzle. The trouble is that much of the information I sought happened so long ago that to ask for a date from three different veterans was to invite three different answers. Even when the answer came straight from the horse's mouth, it would sometimes be wrong. Memories of dates and events have faded with the passing years.

At the end of the book I have listed all the artists who have illustrated any significant quantity' of pinballs since World War II. Unfortunately, I have not been able to include the names of several artists who did the occasional one-off piece of artwork, like the young man who painted the beautiful *Spanish Eyes* for Williams in 1972. Sadly their names have been lost in obscurity.

Throughout I refer to several manufacturers, and an explanation is required for those unfamiliar with the names. For many years pinball manufacturing was dominated by three names: D Gottlieb, Williams, and Bally. Smaller companies include Chicago Coin (called Stern Electronics after 1976), Game Plan (who manufactured from 1978 to 1985), Exhibit and United (two early manufacturers), and Data East (who started pinball production in 1987). All of these companies are or were in the Chicago area. Italian manufacturers include the now defunct Zaccaria, and Mr Game in Bologna.

It would take a Freud or a Jung to explain the appeal of pinball. It is a combination of pitting one's skills and reflexes against a machine that is programmed to beat you, and the visual attractiveness of the graphics that take you into another world. Perhaps it was best summed up by an anonymous philosopher who wrote in 1934: 'Life, sport and pintables have much in common. They are all guided by a combination of skill and luck. Touch and timing are as much the successful combination in the play on pintables as they are in any other sport. An old hand can always beat the novice but both Lion and Rabbit may have the pleasure of seeing a blind shot go home, or the carefully calculated ball just miss its mark and trickle dismally to the "out of play" area.' This is the art of pinball.

KEITH TEMPLE
LONDON 1991

CHAPTER 1

FLASHBACK —
THE ART OF THE BACKFLASH

'THE PINBALL STANDS IN THE CORNER,
SEDUCING WITH LIGHTS AND A BELL,
ENTICING EACH NEW PERFORMER
TO A VISION OF HEAVEN OR HELL.'

PINBALL PARANOIA BY GEOFF HARVEY.

Like some sleazily dressed good-time girl, Madam Pinball, Queen of Darkness, beckons from the shadows attempting to seduce you with her colourful display: 'Play me!' she calls, 'Put some money in the slot for a real good time.' And who could but fail to resist her charms? Mesmerised, you hand over your money and move in close; you put your hands around her waist, press her flipper buttons and you've scored. For a few stolen minutes you are entirely immersed, caressing, shaking, nudging; man and machine locked together in total concentration and involvement. Then the last ball slips out of play and the bonus score racks up in a final climax of flashing lights and digital sounds. You've had your fun; she'll just carry on her trade and

attract the next passer-by. That's the name of her game. Madam Pinball knows no barriers of age, creed, colour or sex. Totally unbigoted, she treats everybody on equal terms. Some get a rougher ride than others but she's always there if you go back for more — better luck next time!

Millions of people from middle-aged businessmen to housewives, teenagers, and schoolboys have been enticed into fooling with Madam Pinball's charms, often the beginning of a lifelong association. Show any five-year-old a pinball for the first time and every instinct tells him this is an object of fun. His eyes widen and light up and he'll run to it, transfixed, hypnotised by its dazzling array of colours and winking lights, his hands reaching out instinctively for the flipper buttons.

An entire team of designers has conspired to create

*LEFT THE GIRL WITH THE FISH IN HER HAIR WAS ORIGINALLY CALLED BARRACUDA, BUT THIS WAS CHANGED TO THE MORE FEMININE NAME, **BARRACORA**. (DOUG WATSON)*

*BELOW BALLY'S **EMBRYON** WAS ORIGINALLY CALLED CLONE. THE GLASS SHOWED EGGS INCUBATING INTO HUMAN BODIES AND CAUSED SOME CONTROVERSY WHEN THE GERMANS ACCUSED ARTIST TONY RAMUNNI OF CREATING A MASTER RACE!*

*LEFT BALLY GAVE AWAY THESE PRINTED PLASTICS TO PROMOTE THEIR 1989 CELEBRITY GAME **ELVIRA**. (GREG FRERES)*

Madam Pinball's glittering facade, giving it the most stunning visual and technical effects to lure the casual adventurer into her grasp. To quote pinball artist Tony Ramunni: 'The artwork is probably the most important part of the machine – it's what people see first and it has to attract them to play the game.' Tony is one of the many talented graphic artists whose skill and artistry is used to weave a theme around the myriad of targets and bumpers taking you on a transport of delight. The journey is into a world of monsters, science-fiction, and travel through space and time, involving you with comic-book superheroes, cowboys and indians, cardsharps, fast cars and even faster women. No longer are you simply playing a humble game of pinball. You can be anything you want to be for the price of a game. This is how Williams advertised their 1987 machine *Fire!*: 'It's hot! It's smokin'! It's burning up the charts! Fire's coming out in a blaze of glory that's firing up play and profits at every location. Just look at the playfield! It actually glows with the heat of the action! Exciting new features like second floor shots and fire escape ramps to save trapped victims... original rag time music and cries for help grab the player in a dramatic rescue scenario. Help! Help! The player must shoot up the fire

escape ramp to rescue an innocent victim.' You can almost feel the heat.

Today's pinball machine has taken 60 years of development and invention. The powerful thumper bumpers, slingshot kickers, spring-loaded plungers, automatic digital scoring and tilt mechanisms are the result of progressive ideas taken from an entire industry, each idea and addition refining and fine-tuning the game's action and appearance. Equally important is the artwork which also has its own history. The sophisticated graphics to *Nitro Groundshaker* or *Dragonfist* would be totally incongruous if applied to a mild action game of the 1930s. Conversely, the colourful but simple art deco motifs used in the 1930s, little more than an embellishment, would be unsuitable on today's state-of-the-art games such as *Heavy Metal Meltdown*. The artwork has developed alongside the action.

Interestingly, pinball art has never tried to influence our tastes but has run parallel to them, informed by our changing social attitudes. This is evident from much of the subject matter used. For instance, ever since the American Civil War the black man was stereotyped as a singing, dancing figure. The fantasy of the 'happy darkie' with his banjo played down the fears of conservative whites.

In 1939 Chicago's Harry Hoppe Corporation brought out a pinball machine called *Taps* which it described in its advertising as follows: 'Animated colored Sambo on the backboard goes into a realistic dance that's a wow! If you ever thrilled to the taps of Fred Astaire or Bill Robinson then funny Sambo will lay you out with laughter.' This idea was still in currency 11 years later, when Gottlieb brought out the *Minstrel Man*. Not only did it feature black minstrels on the playfield and backglass (with eyes that lit up), it actually had three 'Sambo' targets. When hit they dropped, disappeared out of sight, and then popped up again!

Pinball has had other problems with its choice of subject matter. Gottlieb's 1980 machine *Torch* was to celebrate the 1980 Olympic Games due to take place in Moscow. The artwork featured numerous athletes running, jumping, swimming, and fencing while a nubile blonde girl is seen running with the Olympic Torch. There was only one snag. Unfortunately for Gottlieb, America boycotted the olympics as a protest against the Russian invasion of Afghanistan. Bad timing can also cause embarrassment over the choice of a theme. On

GOTTLIEB'S **CORONATION** *WAS RELEASED AT THE HEIGHT OF CORONATION FEVER, SIX MONTHS BEFORE THE CROWNING OF QUEEN ELIZABETH II ON 2ND JUNE 1953. (ROY PARKER)*

ABOVE ARTIST TONY RAMUNNI, NOW CREATIVE DIRECTOR OF MR. GAME IN ITALY, WORKING ON THE ARTWORK TO **MAC ATTACK**.

RIGHT GOTTLIEB'S 1951 **MINSTREL MAN** WITH ITS DROPDOWN "SAMBO" TARGETS WOULD BE UNACCEPTABLE TODAY. A COLLECTABLE MACHINE FROM THE WOOD-RAIL ERA. (ROY PARKER)

LEFT *THE THEME OF FORGOTTEN LANDS INHABITED BY MONSTERS WAS WELL-SUITED TO THE PINBALL FORMAT, AS IN GREG FRERES' 1988 ARTWORK,* **ESCAPE FROM THE LOST WORLD.**

ABOVE *THE STEREOTYPE OF THE SINGING AND DANCING BLACK MAN WAS PERPETUATED BY GOTTLIEB'S MINSTREL MAN IN 1951. (ROY PARKER)*

*THE RELEASE OF WILLIAMS' **EARTHSHAKER** VERY NEARLY COINCIDED WITH THE 1989 SAN FRANCISCO EARTHQUAKE. (TIM ELLIOT)*

the evening of October 17th, 1989, a tremendous earthquake opened up the ground 60 miles south of San Francisco, killing 67 people, injuring 2,400, and leaving 10,000 homeless. Yet only months before Williams Electronics had released its new game *Earthshaker*, based on an earthquake theme. Ironically the management had discussed just this problem at an early stage. As it turned out the slight time gap meant their embarrassment was not as great as it might otherwise have been, despite the sensational advertising and graphics: 'Shoot for the zones the Earthquake Institute has predicted will cause the next quake. Then it's on to The Fault where players will experience an "earthshaker" that tops the Richter Scale. *Earthshaker* shakes, rattles, and rolls as the Institute collapses and California splits from Nevada for a memorable special effect!' The accompanying vivid artwork showed roller-skaters and surfers trying to avoid the advancing splitting ground. One man is being catapulted through the sunroof of his Mercedes while another is being propelled in the air above a jet of water shooting from a broken fire hydrant. He who designs earthquake games certainly stands on shaky ground!

Other problems, however, are not always so easy to foresee. Bally's *Kiss* (featuring the rock group of the same name) spelt the letters 'KISS' across the top of the backglass. Only later was it realised that the angular double 'S' resembled the Nazi SS insignia, and it had to be redesigned for the German market. Incidentally, a similar event happened back in 1934. The British SS Car Company decided its initials were too close for comfort to Hitler's dreaded Schutz Staffel — in 1945 the company was renamed Jaguar Cars Limited.

The war years saw many games adopt beat-the-enemy themes, being given names such as, *Invasion* and *Victorious*. This was later followed by the conquest of space resulting in games entitled *Satellite* and *Friendship 7*. Furthermore, as television came of age, manufacturers started basing games around successful fictional television characters such as *Charlie's Angels* and the *Six Million Dollar Man*. The first film to feature pinball in a big way was *Tommy*, which in turn spawned two classic games from Bally, *Wizard* and *Captain Fantastic*. And as pop music became an established medium, the more enduring of the rock 'n'rollers found their way onto a pinball backglass. The Rolling Stones, Kiss, The Beatles (under the thinly veiled disguise of *The Bootles*), and the King, Elvis Presley, were some of the famous rockers chosen, while the games *Punk* and *Discotek* also got in on the act.

All these pictorial themes could only be shown to their best advantage with a full-size backglass. Although

*STERN'S 1982 GAME **DRAGONFIST** CAPITALISED ON THE POPULARITY OF BRUCE LEE AND THE KUNG FU CRAZE. (DOUG WATSON)*

the early pin games of the 1930s did not have a backbox, it was quickly realised that the potential for a decorative medium was there and by the end of the decade the backbox had almost grown to its present size.

The *Exhibition des Arts Decoratifs*, which was held in Paris in 1925, had been the springboard for a whole lifestyle based on bright colours, geometric designs, and jazzy motifs. Later the term art deco was coined to cover the new look. It influenced everything from fashion to architecture the world over, so naturally its influence spread to the decoration of those early pinball machines. Keeney's *Rainbo* of 1932 was typical with its bold geometric shapes, coloured bright red, yellow, blue, orange, and green. Rockola's *Juggleball* of 1933, while a pre-electric game, used the jazzy electric lightning motif on its playfield and the same bright colours as *Rainbo*. The artwork on the cabinets continued to show this 1930s influence even into the 1960s.

Chromium plating was also a favourite with the art deco stylists, and was used on a whole variety of household items from cigarette lighters to cocktail shakers. It found its way onto the pinball playfield often being used on the sundry metal castings, or it was simulated by the use of highly polished aluminium alloys. The credit for almost the entire output of pinball artwork by Gottlieb and Williams during the post war years until the 1960s goes to two fine artists, Roy Parker and George Molentin. Parker worked on the Gottlieb and Chicago Coin games at an independent screen printing firm called The Reproduction Company in the south-west suburbs of Chicago, while at Advertising Posters Molentin created nearly all the Williams and Bally artwork. It should be remembered that during their peak both Gottlieb and Williams were each producing virtually one new pinball model a month. This kept the artists so busy they had no time to consider whether their art had any social significance or impact. They were simply earning a living doing what they were best at. Both Parker and Molentin survived so long because they were good at their job and provided exactly what the market required.

It has been alleged that Parker sometimes included himself and Gottlieb in the artwork, though most people who worked with him deny this. However, the former Gottlieb game designer Wayne Neyens recalls that 'one

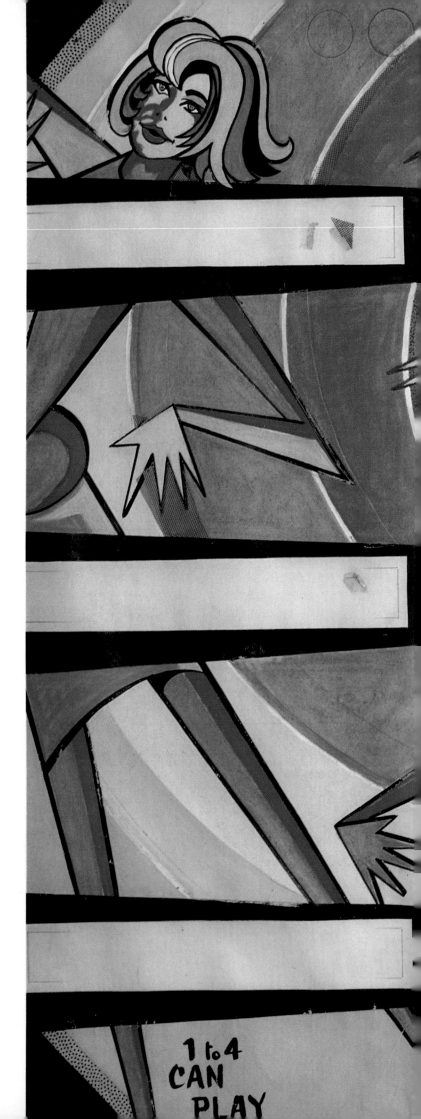

*THE ORIGINAL ARTWORK FOR BALLY'S 1972 **TIME TUNNEL**. FRENCH ARTIST CHRISTIAN MARCHE USED THIS ANGULAR STYLE ON MANY WILLIAMS AND BALLY GAMES IN THE 1960S AND 1970S.*

artist, Gordon Morison, occasionally put people in that he'd worked with though if we caught him we'd make him take it out. Many times he'd sneak someone in without us knowing it. We'd really look for it; I'd catch him once in a while, it was kind of a game. I don't think Parker ever did anything like that, he was too serious.'

Morison was under exclusive contract to design Gottlieb's artwork during the 1970s and early 1980s, and in recalling those days he explains: 'I used to put the names of all my girlfriends in the backglasses; I used to put them in upside down or work them into the hair and the figures and stuff like that. Wayne was looking at a glass upside down one day and that's when he first noticed it so he started looking for them after that. The *Spiderman* backglass has got a couple of girls' names worked into it, and hidden on Princess Ardala's bikini top in *Buck Rogers* is the name 'Sue', a girl I was going out with at the time. It sure impresses a girl to see her name on a pinball machine!'

Sometimes film and pop stars also appeared anonymously on the backglass artwork. A lookalike which did not involve a name was one way of capitalising on a popular contemporary movie or celebrity without incurring licensing problems. Gottlieb's *Gigi* of 1964 featured a Marilyn Monroe figure on the backglass at a time when Marilyn Monroe was in the news following her death. Who knows, perhaps this was in fact Roy Parker's tribute to her. In the 1970s the Italian firm Bell Coinmatics brought out a conversion kit called *The King*. On the glass was the unmistakeable image of Elvis Presley, but there was no direct reference to his name. Another example involves Bell Games which unashamedly used an almost direct copy of the poster for the film *The Terminator*, starring Arnold Schwarzenegger, on its *World Defender* game. The major difference was that on the pinball version the figure was reversed in a mirror image of the film poster.

In the 1970s films based on the exploits of martial arts exponents became very popular, particularly those starring Bruce Lee, the supermaster of Kung Fu. By a clever play on words and pictures *Dragonfist*, by Stern, encompassed the visual flavour of one of Lee's best-known movies, *Enter the Dragon*. The game featured a lookalike Bruce Lee fighting off several attackers at once, his muscles rippling just as they did in real life. Bally, on the other hand, ran into a little trouble from the producers of *Happy Days* when their artist Paul Faris used a Fonz lookalike on the backglass of *Eight Ball* in 1977. (Fonz was the lead character in the hugely successful TV Show *Happy Days*.) That kind of accusation can never be proved of course, and *Eight Ball*

became the all-time best-selling pinball game, selling over 20,000 machines.

Incidentally, the producers of *Happy Days* are not above making mistakes themselves. Although the series was supposedly set around 1960, the pinball in the local diner scene was a *Nip-It*, a 1973 machine ironically made by Bally. Another example of pinball 'time-warping' was in the film *American Graffiti* which was supposedly set in 1962 and contained several pinballs, including a 1965 Gottlieb's *Buckaroo* and worse still, a 1971 Bally *Vampire* – nine years before its time!

It is not generally appreciated how prolific the manufacturers of pinball machines have been over the years. Competition is such that to rest on one's pinball laurels is to invite stagnation. Consequently, the various manufacturers between them have introduced well over 1,000 different designs since World War II. Gottlieb has certainly been prolific bringing out an average of one new model per month since this time, only slowing up during the video 'invasion' around 1980. Williams' average is not far behind. And what unites the diverse themes is a hint of excitement or adventure, with the titles gradually becoming more macho and aggressive as the years passed by.

SIX MILLION DOLLAR MAN WAS A SIX-PLAYER GAME FROM BALLY. (PAUL FARIS)

Prospector, Challenger, Fairground, Silver Skates, St Moritz, and *Yacht Club* were all typical names of early games in the 1930s. Even up until the 1960s the names had not changed very much, although the themes were becoming more topical. *Beatniks* (1967), *Psychedelic* (1970), *World Fair* (1964), *Discotek* (1965), *Satellite* (1958), *Apollo* (1967), and *Moonshot* (1969) all echo something of their era and an obvious dawning of the space age. Film spin-offs were certainly another factor in pinball's history. In 1971 Bally brought out *Four Million BC*, using a theme based on a land of prehistoric monsters. The movie *One Million Years BC* which starred Raquel Welch, had been released in 1966, and the pinball backglass, painted by Dick White, closely resembled the original film poster in its design, except that Raquel Welch is unfortunately missing in the pinball version! Both depicted a rampant dinosaur encountering a stegosaurus.

Another film spin-off, in addition to *Wizard* and *Captain Fantastic*, was Bally's *Flicker* (1975) which had

an attractive glass mainly featuring Laurel and Hardy with smaller cameo pictures of WC Fields, Edward G Robinson, and Humphrey Bogart. Then, in 1982, came *Rocky* – based on the successful series of movies of the same name starring Sylvester Stallone – and in 1978 *Close Encounters. Close Encounters of the Third Kind* was the 1977 story of a series of UFOs landing in Indiana. Since this was a Columbia picture, with Columbia now owning Gottlieb, it is no surprise that the latter brought out this particular title in 1978.

Television series provided another range of spin-offs. Gottlieb pioneered the way with *Charlie's Angels* (1978), based on the popular 1970s series starring Farah Fawcett-Majors, Kate Jackson, and Jaclyn Smith

THE ORIGINAL ARTWORK FOR A PROPOSED GAME BASED ON 1970S FASHION. THE GAME WAS NEVER PRODUCED BUT THE MODIFIED ARTWORK WAS USED ON WILLIAMS' **SWINGER** IN 1972. (CHRISTIAN MARCHE)

as three intrepid and glamorous female detectives under the command of the disembodied voice of their boss, Charlie. During the 1970s everyone started going licence crazy, particularly Bally. Tom Nieman, in the marketing department, came up with a pinball version of the *Six Million Dollar Man* in 1978, again based on a popular television series, this time featuring the bionic man, Steve Austin, played by the non-bionic Lee Majors. With Lee then married to Farah Fawcett-Majors this was probably the first husband and wife team to make a pinball appearance.

Dr David Banner was another television character who, in 1979, metamorphosed onto a pinball glass. He was a scientist trying to tap into the hidden strengths that all humans apparently possess. Unfortunately an overdose of gamma radiation altered his body chemistry, so that the 'Incredible Hulk' appeared whenever he became angry, splitting his shirt and trousers on each occasion! 'Don't make me angry' Banner used to say, 'You wouldn't like me when I'm angry!' *The Incredible Hulk* had an attractive backglass painted by Gordon Morison and showed Banner going through the different stages of his metamorphosis. Gordon had to travel to New York to have the drawings approved by Marvel Comics, the copyright holders.

The 1970s gave pinball a real shot in the arm. During the previous decade Bally had produced some instantly forgettable games, but the introduction of new blood into the company revolutionised the direction in which pinball was going. *Capersville* (1966), *The Wiggler* (1967) and *Four Million BC* (1971) all started a new trend in unusual game designs. For instance they

featured the multi-ball, whereby up to three balls could be used simultaneously on hitting the correct targets. Another novelty was the zipper flipper. This was unique to Bally, and consisted of a mechanism whereby two flippers would move together and narrow the gap between them. Again this was performed by hitting certain targets, usually a mushroom bumper: the flippers would remain closed until a ball hit another mushroom bumper whereupon they opened. Obviously the player tried to avoid hitting this particular bumper, but with three balls careering off in all directions it was difficult and fun.

Capersville was a best-seller and marked a change of direction in pinball graphics. It utilised the talents of Jerry K Kelley and introduced a jazzy, modernist style of artwork that was very different to the traditional comic art, a style he had first used on Williams *Pot o' Gold*. Bally's *Four Million BC*, however, returned to the traditional style with a theme of prehistoric monsters yet even here there was a novel plunger shot, whereby the ball was fired across the centre of the playfield instead of round the top as had occurred for decades, ensuring considerable success for this particular game.

During the 1970s Bally was the name of the game. In 1972 the company hit the artistic jackpot with its *Fireball*. Designed by Ted Zale, *Fireball* not only had multi-ball and zipper flippers but an unusual plunger shot in which the ball had to roll up a ramp. In addition there was a messenger ball whereby the ball in play could hit a ball held captive in a narrow alley, the energy being transferred from one to the other sending the captive up the alley to score. The designers *pièce-de-*

ABOVE BELL COINMATICS OF ITALY PRODUCED MAINLY CONVERSION KITS FOR BALLY GAMES. **THE KING** WAS THEIR FIRST ('MIKE'). **RIGHT BEATNIKS** WAS A PRODUCT OF THE SWINGING SIXTIES. THE FLAKING AREAS SEEN ON THIS MACHINE ARE USUALLY CAUSED BY DAMP.

WHEN ADVERTISING POSTERS NEEDED SOMEONE TO REPLACE ROY PARKER IN THE 1960S, ART STENHOLM DID SO ADMIRABLY, AS ILLUSTRATED BY THIS HUMOROUS DETAIL FROM WILLIAMS' CLASSIC 1964 GAME **HEATWAVE**.

ABOVE *FIRST COLOUR ROUGH FOR BALLY'S 1987 **HEAVY METAL MELTDOWN**. (TONY RAMUNNI)*

RIGHT *FINAL ROUGH COLOUR SKETCH FOR **HEAVY METAL MELTDOWN**. NOTE THE REFINEMENTS FROM THE PREVIOUS SKETCH. (TONY RAMUNNI)*

résistance, though, was a spinning flat disc, a few inches in diameter and flush with the playfield surface, which would send the ball careering off in unpredictable directions, an idea recently revived by Williams on the *Whirlwind* which had *three* spinning discs on the playfield.

What really set this game head and shoulders above the rest was the stunning artwork. The creator was Bally's new talented young artist, David Christensen, who gave arguably his best shot to this, his first ever pinball. The backglass had a dark blue background and centre stage was an apocalyptic red devil hurling fireballs towards the player. Christensen recalls how he had been working freelance for Bally's engineering department doing the exploded diagrams and text for its service manuals. 'In 1971 as a sideline experiment I drew my first machine, *Fireball*. The game was such a success that I became hard pressed to provide Bally with both service manuals and new game designs. With additional help I was able to concentrate my time on my

first love, art and design. I thought I'd try and compete with the art department there, who were still doing fairly traditional stuff like *Vampire* and *Nip-It*.'

While not Bally's highest ever seller, *Fireball* was a great favourite with players who agreed it was like nothing they had played before. Twenty years on it is still highly prized by collectors. In later years, *Fireball II*, *Fireball Classic*, and a special *Fireball* for home use were produced by Bally, all based on Christensen's original

BELOW AND RIGHT *THE ITALIAN CONVERSION KIT,* **WORLD DEFENDER** *BORE MORE THAN A PASSING RESEMBLANCE TO THE FILM POSTER FOR THE TERMINATOR.*

All you have to do is mount our kit on your own Bally - any model

Hemdale Pre
Arnold Schwar
Effetti Speciali
Produttore Esecutivo Jc
ORION PICTURES Release
Proc

CHWARZENEGGER

RMINATOR

nta Una Produzione Pacific Western di un Film di James Cameron
egger "Terminator" Michael Biehn, Linda Hamilton e Paul Winfield
cco di Stan Winston · Direttore della Fotografia Adam Greenberg
Daly e Derek Gibson · Scritto da James Cameron
o da Gale Anne Hurd · Diretto da James Cameron con Gale Anne Hurd

HOT FUN

IN 1980 BALLY'S **SKATEBALL** INCORPORATED ALL THE EXCITEMENT OF THE SKATEBOARD CRAZE. (GREG FRERES)

CHAMPION OF THE GAMES

Gottlieb's **TORCH**

ABOVE
THE 1980 OLYMPICS WAS THE THEME FOR **TORCH**, WHICH DISPLAYS THE AMERICAN FLAG. HOWEVER, AMERICA BOYCOTTED THE GAMES IN PROTEST OVER RUSSIA'S INVASION OF AFGHANISTAN. (GORDON MORISON)

HOT LICKS
Bally Midway amplifies your earnings with the high energy pinball excitement of HEAVY METAL MELTDOWN!

RIGHT 'IF IT'S TOO LOUD YOU'RE TOO OLD'.
HEAVY METAL MELTDOWN HAD 'AWESOME STACKS' SURMOUNTING THE BACKBOX. (TONY RAMUNNI)

artwork. The age of the circus clown and comic character backglass had been firmly laid to rest. The macho image had arrived. The trend continued through to the 1980s and up to the present with action-packed themes and action-packed names: *Nitro Groundshaker*, *Spy Hunter*, *Karate Fight*, *Heavy Metal Meltdown*, *Dragonfist*, *Firepower* and *Cyclone* being typical of recent titles.

Inevitably, with so many hundreds of different pinball machines being manufactured, the names of many machines were repeated. The circus motif, always popular on earlier machines, gave the name *Big Top* to at least three different models by Pioneer (1945), Genco (1949), and Gottlieb (1964). The name *Circus* was used on at least five machines by Genco (1949), Exhibit (1948), United (1952), and by Bally (in 1932 and 1973). Gottlieb had *Super Circus* (1957) and *Flying Circus* (1961), but Williams seems to have almost completely avoided the sawdust ring, coming nearest to it in 1955 with *Circus Wagon*. *Carnival* was another popular name, appearing on at least three models by

Bally, Midway, and Sega. Other names used at least twice include: *South Pacific*, *Moon-Shot*, *Zig-Zag*, *Trade Winds*, *Double Feature*, *Champ*, *Golden Gloves*, *Airport*, *Spirit of '76*, *Bonanza*, *Harvest*, *Knockout*, and *Flicker*.

Names with a hint of royalty have always been popular too, particularly when linked with card games. Hence Gottlieb's *Card King* (1971), Bally's *King Tut* (1969) based on the Egyptian pharaoh Tutankhamun, and a palace full of kings and queens – *Bowling Queen*, *Gipsy Queen*, *4 Queens*, *Kings and Queens*, *Queen of Diamonds*, *Jungle King*, *King Rock*, *Sky Kings*, and so on. The British Royal Family has always been of great interest to Americans and Europeans alike, which is why Gottlieb brought out *Coronation* in 1953 to coincide with the crowning of Queen Elizabeth II. The artist Roy Parker cheekily depicted a pretty young girl wearing a crown, looking more like Miss World than Queen Elizabeth! In 1969 Gottlieb produced *Royal Guard* showing London's famous changing of the guard ceremony with the guardsmen wearing their red tunics and the famous bearskin helmets.

In the very early days of pinball even Humpty Dumpty became a pinball character. So, when Gottlieb's post-war production resumed, *Humpty Dumpty* (1947) had the distinction of being the first game to be fitted with flippers. So successful was the machine that Gottlieb sold 6,500 at a time when the average production run was between 500 and 1,000. Clearly *Humpty Dumpty* was all that he was cracked up to be! Gottlieb followed this up with a straight run of children's nursery rhyme themes through 1948 – *Lady Robin Hood*, *Cinderella*, *Jack and Jill*, *King Cole*, *Ali Baba*, *Alice in Wonderland* and *Barnacle Bill*. A few card games and bowling themes broke the run until *The Three Musketeers* and *King Arthur* appeared in 1949. Captain Kidd, who had appeared on a machine by ABT Manufacturing in 1936, reappeared under the Gottlieb banner in 1960. Artist Roy Parker mischievously depicted Captain Kidd as a curvy young lady showing off her treasure chest.

During the 1950s and early 1960s Gottlieb and Williams' were almost working to a formula. Month after month a new machine would appear from each manufacturer. The Gottlieb machine would carry Roy Parker's artwork and the Williams would have George Molentin's, both featuring pretty girls and comic characters. Everything in the garden was rosy, life was sweet and everyone thought that the good times would last forever.

SKETCH FOR A PROPOSED GAME BASED ON THE TELEVISION SERIES AND COMIC BOOK, *THE LONE RANGER*; THE GAME WAS NEVER MANUFACTURED. (GORDON MORISON)

CHAPTER 2
LOOKING BACK –
BAGATELLES AND BUMPERS

'PINBALL PAUL BEATS THEM ALL, GETS 10,000 EVERY BALL,
PULLS BACK THE JIGGER, GIVES IT A TWIST,
LETS IT GO – HE'S NEVER MISSED.
WHEN PINBALL PAUL GETS THE CALL, EVERY RECORD STARTS TO FALL,
SHOOTS WITH HIS EYES CLOSED HALF THE TIME,
PLAYS ALL DAY FOR ONLY A DIME.'

PINBALL PAUL – GLENN MILLER & HIS ORCHESTRA (1939).

THIS LONDON AMUSEMENT ARCADE IN THE 1930S DISPLAYS A GOOD SELECTION OF EARLY PINBALL MACHINES.

BALLY'S 1982 BROCHURE RECREATED THE ATMOSPHERE OF FAT SAM'S SPEAKEASY IN BUGSY MALONE.

In October 1929 the infamous Wall Street Crash wiped millions off the value of stocks and shares overnight, and the fall continued for three years. The Crash was caused by a great surge of speculation. Many people lost everything they owned. Over 5,000 banks closed and unemployment soared from 2 to nearly 15 million, about a quarter of the workforce. With no unemployment pay, poverty was severe. Many had to hunt for food in dustbins, while some even tried to get themselves arrested because a gaol was at least warm and dry and provided food. Queues for bread and coal formed in every American city.

Great Britain, which had been getting back onto its feet after the General Strike of 1926, was also plunged into recession, along with the whole of Europe. 'Buddy, can you spare a dime?' was not limited to America. Many struggling businesses gladly paid out $16 or so for a small pinball game which would sit on the counter. It enticed people into the store where, hopefully, they might buy a few goods. The new pin games quickly paid for themselves.

Several Americans had been working independently on a coin-operated version of the old-fashioned baga-

*RIGHT THE 1930S PINBALL CRAZE LED TO INCREASED INTEREST IN HOME BAGATELLE GAMES LIKE LINDSTROM'S BEAUTIFULLY DECORATED **NESTING BIRDS**.*

telle game. They had quickly realised that games pitting a player's skill against a machine were the most popular. Arthur L. Paulin and Earl W. Froom had invented one such game early in 1931. It was called *Whiffle* and gave 10 balls for a nickel. A few prototypes on location proved it was a real money-spinner and they were soon producing over 100 games a day. Around the same time the *Whoopee* game, made by Chicago's In and Out-door Games Company, was apparently making profits of $15 – $20 a day based on 5 cents for 10 balls. In the advertisements one hotel owner claimed to have taken $201.20 in 12½ days – and this was during a severe recession.

David Gottlieb had been a small-time entrepreneur during the 1920s. He travelled round the Texas oilfields making a few bucks from the oil men by playing a version of lucky dip, a fortunate worker taking a slip of paper signifying a prize. In 1927 Gottlieb moved to Chicago, manufacturing various machines, and three years later he moved to a larger factory in Chicago needing new products to survive. He then started to manufacture a game called Bingo in conjunction with another Chicago game manufacturer, Jack Keeney. Problems with a patent issued by the Bingo Novelty

*BELOW ROCKOLA'S 1933 **JUGGLEBALL** INTRODUCED A MOVEABLE ROD TO GIVE THE PLAYER SOME BALL CONTROL. ALTHOUGH THIS WAS A PRE-ELECTRIC GAME, IT USED THE POPULAR LIGHTNING MOTIF IN THE ARTWORK.*

*DAVID GOTTLIEB'S 1931 BEST-SELLING **BAFFLE BALL** WAS THE FIRST OF HUNDREDS OF PINBALL MACHINES WHICH TOOK THE NAME GOTTLIEB TO THE FOREFRONT OF PINBALL MANUFACTURE.*

Company spurred Gottlieb to bring out another game all his own. In 1931 he issued *Baffle Ball*. It measured only 24 x 16 inches, taking up little room on a counter top. It was incredibly popular. At peak production Gottlieb was making 400 *Baffle Ball* machines a day, selling 50,000 of them in under a year. Thirty people worked around the clock to meet the demand, probably an all-time production record. At this time there was little or no artwork or decoration, the emphasis being placed more on the quality of the polished wooden cabinet and chrome plated fittings. The playfield was finished in a rich green paint with gold diamond decoration and lettering, and golden metal pins.

One of Gottlieb's distributors, the Lion Manufacturing Company, found Gottlieb could not supply them fast enough to fill all the orders. A junior partner in the company, Ray Moloney, decided to fill the gap by manufacturing his own machines. Moloney was an adventurous person willing to take risks, and always listened to inventors who came to him with their seemingly crazy ideas. The name of his first machine was *Ballyhoo*. 'What'll they do through 32? – play

Ballyhoo', quipped the colourful advertising literature. Moloney had seen a risque satirical magazine on a newstand one day and was struck by the bright attractive cover. He lifted the design and used it on the playfield of his new game, the brightly coloured diamond patterns being much more eyecatching than the walnut and green paint used on Gottlieb's *Baffle Ball*. Moloney also unashamedly used the name of the magazine for his pinball game, and even called his new company the Bally Manufacturing Company. Using his nationwide contacts Moloney sold around 75,000 *Ballyhoos* for about $16.50 each.

With the pinball industry booming dozens of small backyard 'factories' began turning out simple games. Many unemployed engineers and inventors from the big factories which were closing down turned their talents to striking it rich with a popular pin game. Meanwhile, the humble bagatelle, which was the forerunner of the pinball machine, was also enjoying a revival for home use.

As the industry developed so the artwork became ever more sophisticated, moving from simple geometric designs to themes. In 1932 *Pla-Girl* tried to charm its predominantly male audience with bathing beauties.

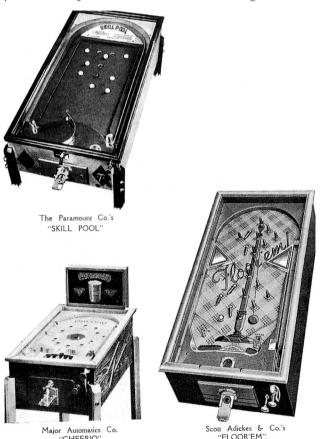

Meet—
"THE BUMPER"
—by BALLY.
● The Latest Scott-Adickes Winner ●

Giant Coil-springs keep ball moving like a Footer game.

THE "BUMPER" never lacks players because interest is sustained till last ball fades out.

LOOKS AN EASY MONEY GAME. BUT BEST SCORES ARE FROM SKILL-PLAY.
*
Proclaimed the finest table game at the CHICAGO EXHIBITION last month and LONDON. D O I N MACHINE EXHIBITION.

PLUG IN TO MAINS. NO ACCUMULATORS. NO BATTERIES. NO POCKETS OR PINS

12 Electrified Coil-springs keep Balls bump-, bump-, bumping and scoring

The great fascination of BUMPER lies in its amazing Springs and Ball action.

SCOTT, ADICKES & Co., Ltd.,
34 - 35, FURNIVAL STREET, LONDON, E.C.4
Telephone: Holborn 9421-2-3.

BALLY'S BUMPER WAS THE FIRST TO USE ELECTRIFIED SPRING BUMPERS WHICH REPLACED THE OLDER MECHANICAL SCORING METHODS.

The Paramount Co.'s "SKILL POOL"

Major Automatics Co. "CHEERIO"

Scott Adickes & Co.'s "FLOOR'EM"

THREE EARLY PINTABLES DESIGNED FOR LICENSED PREMISES. SKILL POOL HAD A MOVEABLE ARM WHICH GAVE THE PLAYER SOME SKILL CONTROL.

THE AUTOMATIC WORLD & AMUSEMENT CATERER

August, 1934.

TELL THE WORLD!

How much the Automatic Machine Trade helps to Reduce Unemployment and Fight Depression.

Rockolas' *Jigsaw* in 1933 had a mechanical jigsaw puzzle on the playfield. By manoeuvering the ball into selected holes a scene from the 1933 Chicago World's Fair was assembled. *Jigsaw* was the first game to be exported to Europe in any quantity, with Britain taking over 60 per cent of the exports. Interestingly, one amusement arcade in England is still operating several of these *Jigsaws*, the arcade owner having bought them new in 1933 for £18 each.

Scott, Adickes Games are Better !

The Brother of the Criss-Cross Alite is—

SCORE-ALITE

GENCO BRINGS YOU TWIN PLUNGERS.

Score-Alite makes a clever use of the famous Lite-up Unit. The 10 holes on the playing field have corresponding lights on the back flash. The 1,000, 900, 800, 700 and 600 lights must be lit to win—with greater rewards for each successive light. Double action and double interest is created by having an additional plunger on the left side to shoot balls that otherwise would be obvious "outs". The richly coloured playing field and de luxe cabinet make a most beautiful ensemble. : : :

THE GREATEST OF THE BEST

WHIRPOOL TICKET MACHINE

STARLITE
The Machine with a Future
A NEW Game, with NEW Features & NEW Thrills.

SCOTT, ADICKES & CO. LTD.,
BANK CHAMBERS, 329 HIGH HOLBORN, LONDON, W.C.I.

A 1935 ADVERTISEMENT FOR AMERICAN PINTABLES IMPORTED INTO BRITAIN. NOTE THE EARLY USE OF THE ILLUMINATED BACKFLASH.

The big advantage of the British market was that the same player instructions and repair manuals could be used, with only a different coin mechanism being required. It was not long before British games were being turned out, very often as blatant copies of the American originals. The *Aurora Super-De-Luxe*, for instance, was an exact copy of Keeney's *Rainbo*. Meanwhile on the west coast of America another distributor of coin-operated machines, Harry Williams, decided to make his own games. Williams had decided that more action was needed on the playfield. Apparently his workshop was next to a small electrical factory which used devices called solenoids. (A solenoid is a coil of wire which when energised with electricity can pull a plunger through its hollow centre and activate mechanical devices.) After experimenting Williams knew the future lay with electricity and released the first electrical pinball game, *Contact*, in 1932. Of all the advances in the history of the game this was the most significant,

and the game was transformed overnight.

A second big advance at this time came with the repeal of prohibition in America in 1933, which meant people could legally have a drink and play pinball at the same time! Roosevelt said, 'I think this would be a good time for a beer.' It was also a good time for pinball. In England, amusement trade papers began complaining about the flood of new games coming over from America.

After exhibiting *Contact* at the big annual Chicago Fair, the other manufacturers jumped onto the bandwagon, with several adding lights, albeit on the playfield. Two years later the first backbox appeared. Set vertically at right angles to the playfield, Genco's *Criss Cross* had one just a few inches high, but big enough for the score to be easily read. The artwork, however, was still minimal, consisting of simple coloured embellishments. Meanwhile the crude batteries of the earlier machines were replaced by mains transformers.

RIGHT THIS SMALL PINTABLE WAS BASED ON THE FAMOUS FLYING SCOT EXPRESS TRAIN WHICH HELD THE NON-STOP LONDON TO EDINBURGH RECORD IN 1928.

" Look alive, Here's the Flood"!
* * * *

ABOVE THIS IS HOW ONE 1930S AMUSEMENT TRADE PAPER SAW THE FLOOD OF IMPORTED AMERICAN PINTABLES INTO GREAT BRITAIN.

In 1937 Bally invented a spring bumper, another invention that marked a major advance in pinball technology, and brought out its *Bumper* game. *Bumper* was different because you scored by hitting a ball into the electrified springs in the bumpers instead of having the ball fall into a hole. This is how one 1937 trade newspaper reviewed it:

Bump — Bump — Bump — Bumper! This is what happens on Bumper, a new Bally table game, after the steel ball is catapulted into play. There are a dozen 1.5 inch diameter coil springs where normally there would be pins and holes. The fascinating antics of the ball caused by the cuffs and kicks it gets from the coil springs with which it continuously collides would be desperately irritating but for the fact that every kick sends the score up to 10 points, and it is not unusual for the same ball to return three or four times to the same coil spring for more. Bumper is

drawing big crowds everywhere and is easily 'the hit of the season'.

The backglass too had developed and grown considerably in size during the late 1930s, manufacturers realising that here was a way of attracting people to the machines by the use of attractive artwork. The scene was set for the modern pinball machine as we know it. Only one major advance was missing (the flipper). And then came Pearl Harbour. After the Japanese air force attacked the American fleet on December 7th, 1941, the entire amusement industry converted to war production. Genco manufactured cores for armour-piercing shells, and anti-radar systems, and Gottlieb made mainly small metal parts for parachute harnesses and bombs.

BELOW

TURF CHAMPS WAS A PAYOUT PINTABLE. THIS TYPE OF GAMBLING PINTABLE LED TO A CLAMP DOWN ON ALL PINBALL MACHINES BY THE AUTHORITIES.

ABOVE *THE ARTWORK FOR GENCO'S JUNIOR SHOWS THE INFLUENCE OF THE ART DECO MOVEMENT AND FEATURES ELECTRIC SPRING BUMPERS WHICH SCORED AUTOMATICALLY ON THE BACKGLASS.*

Although the demand for pin-games was as great as ever, no new machines were being made. Instead Harry Williams and his electrical engineer, Lyn Durant, set up a company called the United Manufacturing Company to refurbish old pinball machines. 'You'll get and hold the play, with games revamped the United way', ran the advertisements. Since they could not get hold of any new materials, not even the essential solder, they had to strip down the worst of the machines and melt out the old solder for re-use. They re-screenprinted the artwork on the playfield and glass with new designs, usually on a patriotic war theme, and soon other manufacturers joined the refurbishing bandwagon. Stoner's *Turf Champ* was converted to *Victorious 1943* and *Invasion*,

*GENCO'S **AIRPORT** IS A PARTICULARLY ATTRACTIVE PERIOD GLASS WITH ITS PROPELLOR DRIVEN PLANES AND AIRSHIP, CAPTURING THE LEISURELY PACE OF A LATE 1930S AIRPORT. (ROY PARKER)*

but the prize for imagination must go to Victory Games for its conversion of *Genco's Ten Spot* to the wonderful *Smack the Japs*, a theme the car industry endorsed 40 years later! Anti-Japanese sentiment unashamedly ran right through the whole arcade games industry, with many having such titles as: *Klip-a-Nip*, *Tokyo Raider*, *Jap Sky Fighter*, as well as *Hit the Jap*, *Slap the Jap*, and even *Sink the Jap*.

Normality quickly returned after the war and a new dimension soon hit the pinball world. Hitherto, the skill in pinball had been in the initial plunger shot, followed by nudging and pushing the machine to try and propel the ball along the desired trajectory. In the famous St Louis Freeplay game case, one witness demonstrated in court the high degree of skill that could be attained by the player on these basic machines by the judicious use of the plunger. One newspaper report stated: 'The witness demonstrated that he could select certain pins to be struck on various parts of the board and in two trials was able to hit two out of the three pins selected.'

LOCATION TESTED... ALL THE THRILLS OF REAL GOLF!

Williams' MINI·GOLF

2-PLAYER

the first realistic 9-hole putting green under glass!

a real test of putting skill

- Player turns "Mini Golfer" toward lighted hole
- Player can control "Mini Golfer's" stroke with "hard stroke" or "easy stroke" button.
- Each player "putts" alternately, hole by hole, until all 9 holes are made or 27 strokes used.

buy the best—buy williams

- Formica Playfield and Front Molding
- Stainless Steel Trim Cabinet
- Single or Twin Chutes (slug rejectors)

*ABOVE WILLIAMS' **MINI-GOLF** FEATURED A MINIATURE GOLF COURSE AND MANIKIN*

THE RARE USE OF CYCLING AS A THEME IS SEEN ON THIS PRE-WAR BACKGLASS. THE CYCLE TRACK IS IN FACT AN EARLY EXAMPLE OF A MIRRORED FINISH.

BELOW DETAIL FROM **SKI-HI**, WHICH USED
A BACKLIT SKIER PROGRESSIVELY MOVING
DOWN THE SKI JUMP.

RIGHT RED INDIAN FUN AND GAMES FROM ROY
PARKER IN THIS GOTTLIEB MACHINE FROM 1953,
POKER FACE.

BELOW THE WILD WEST WAS A POPULAR THEME. THIS GAME FROM UNITED IN 1950 IS ONE OF THE LARGE NUMBER ILLUSTRATED BY GEORGE MOLENTIN.

RIGHT COWBOYS AND INDIANS ENGAGE IN A VIOLENT SHOOT-OUT IN THIS 1951 GAME FROM GOTTLIEB. (ROY PARKER)

Such skills were soon to become obsolete.

In 1947 a Gottlieb designer Harry Mabs had the idea of introducing a small arm, powered by solenoids, and operated by a button on each side of the cabinet. The world's first pinball machine with flippers was the game *Humpty Dumpty*. As with other great inventions, such as the telephone and the television, it is probable that several people had the same idea at the same time,

because within a month of *Humpty Dumpty's* introduction Chicago Coin had brought out *Bermuda* with flippers, and in no time all new pinball games included them. Conversion kits immediately came onto the market to convert the older pre-flipper games which had now become obsolete.

The flipper revolutionised the game. What was surprising was that no-one had thought of it sooner

*GUYS AND GALS EYE EACH OTHER IN A DETAIL FROM WILLIAMS' 1961 GAME **HIGHWAYS**. THE PERIOD STYLING OF THE CARS AND CLOTHES IS BY GEORGE MOLENTIN.*

because baseball games, using a small flipper-like bat controlled by a button or lever on the front of the machine, had been on the market for several years. Yet nobody thought of applying this mechanism to pinball. *Humpty Dumpty* had a rather generous supply of six flippers three to each side of the cabinet. Steve Kordek, manager of Pinball Design at Williams Electronics explained, 'The flipper was the making of the pinball game. It gave the game respectability, and added the skill element, anywhere up to 90 per cent depending on the design.' Kordek went on to compliment himself on being the first person to design a game with the two flippers positioned as they are today: 'In the Chicago Show at the Sherman Hotel in January 1948 every one else had copied *Humpty Dumpty* and had six flippers — I had two at the bottom of the playfield where they have been ever since. I'm very very proud of that accomplishment.' Originally they pointed outwards but by 1951 they pointed inwards at the bottom of the field.

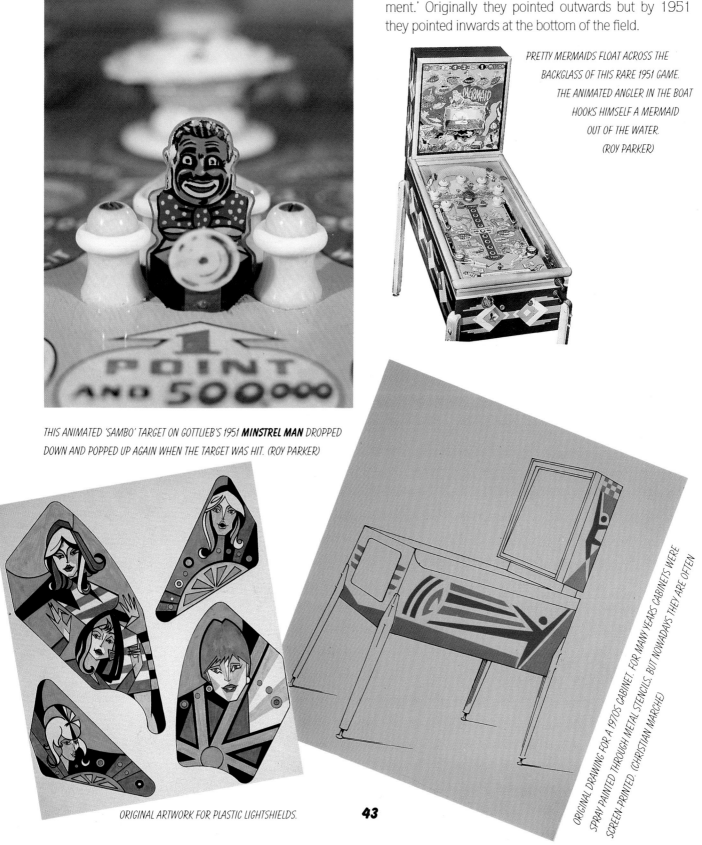

PRETTY MERMAIDS FLOAT ACROSS THE BACKGLASS OF THIS RARE 1951 GAME. THE ANIMATED ANGLER IN THE BOAT HOOKS HIMSELF A MERMAID OUT OF THE WATER. (ROY PARKER)

*THIS ANIMATED 'SAMBO' TARGET ON GOTTLIEB'S 1951 **MINSTREL MAN** DROPPED DOWN AND POPPED UP AGAIN WHEN THE TARGET WAS HIT. (ROY PARKER)*

ORIGINAL ARTWORK FOR PLASTIC LIGHTSHIELDS.

ORIGINAL DRAWING FOR A 1970S CABINET. FOR MANY YEARS CABINETS WERE SPRAY-PAINTED THROUGH METAL STENCILS, BUT NOWADAYS THEY ARE OFTEN SCREEN-PRINTED. (CHRISTIAN MARCHE)

CHAPTER 3
THE ROCK 'N' ROLL YEARS

By the mid-1950s youth, the biggest consumer of pinball, had a new name, The Teenager. Young people now had their own group identity, their own dress (turned-up blue denim jeans and pointed shoes), hairstyles, and music. Both in Europe and America there was a new generation with more money to spend than ever before. In coffee bars and diners they drank frothy Italian coffee or Coca-Cola and listened to pop music on chrome-finned jukeboxes. And they played pinball. In the home, too, there were developments. Television was rapidly overtaking the radio as the number one entertainment medium turning nations of listeners into a more visually oriented audience. Meanwhile, advertising explored this trend using more pictures and less text. And for the new visually aware teenager nothing could be more appealing than the beckoning glow and brightly coloured imagery of the pinball machine.

The pinball machines of the 1950s are now regarded by the world's pinball collectors as the product of 'the Golden Age of Pinball'. All the key ingredients of the modern game were in place – the flippers, slingshot kickers, and pop bumpers – and they remained right to the present day. The cabinets at this time still featured

*FIVE COLLECTABLE CLASSICS. THE OLDEST IS THE 1958 GOTTLIEB **CRISS-CROSS** ON THE EXTREME RIGHT.*

*A HUMOROUS DETAIL BY ART STENHOLM ON THE BACKGLASS OF GOTTLIEB'S **KING OF DIAMONDS** IN 1967.*

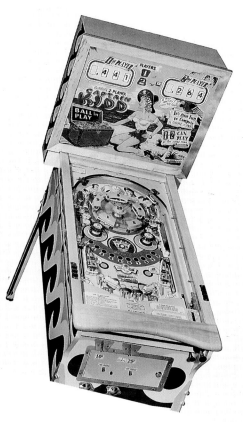

attractive, varnished, natural-wood side rails, backglass surrounds, and legs. Like the radio cabinets of the same period these machines projected an image of well-constructed solid dependability. But by 1960 this image changed. The impending age of the vandal meant armour-plating was needed in the form of stainless steel side rails.

The artwork of the 1950s, both on the backglass and playfield, was attractive. It was interesting, too, because a closer examination often revealed many small touches of subtle humour. There was additional charm in the way the scores were indicated. There were no reels and instead a bulb would light behind the relevant total which was printed on the backglass. This meant the artist had to use considerable ingenuity to incorporate the score numbers into the artwork which made the machines even more visually appealing. Furthermore, since the customers were predominantly male the illustrations also featured pretty girls. Pinball art, like the cinema poster and the magazine cover, has always tried to exploit the male fixation with the well-endowed female body of a Marilyn Monroe, Jane Russell, or Jayne Mansfield.

Whatever the game's theme the pretty girl was there. In Gottlieb's 1959 *Racetime*, depicting horse racing on the glass, the dream girl sits in the corner holding her binoculars while on the playfield are a couple of pinball beauties dressed as jockeys. A more extreme version is Gottlieb's *Paradise*, which had Hawaiian girls dancing and smiling over the entire machine. But by the mid-1960s pinball artwork had to alter to survive. It could not subsist on a never-ending diet of clowns and pretty girls. Youth culture was becoming more sophisticated with Mary Quant revolutionising teenage fashion,

Vidal Sassoon reshaping hairstyles, and a new generation of photographers deifying teenage fashion and beauty. And on top of that the psychedelic age had arrived. Teenagers were experimenting with amphetamines and LSD and one dress shop in trendy Chelsea even called itself 'Granny Takes a Trip', an obvious reference to the use of hallucinogenic drugs.

The pinball artists responded to the new youth culture with game titles such as *Beatniks*, *Discotek*, *Psychedelic*, *Beat Time*, *Jive Time* and *Rock 'n' Roll*. However the manufacturers seemed to resent too much change because it was not until the 1970s that the artistic approach showed any great change. Perhaps the reason was that virtually every pinball machine produced since the war had its artwork created by one of two men, Roy Parker or George Molentin. An artist's style is a kind of handwriting and it is not something that can be easily changed. Parker and Molentin's styles were still largely rooted in their artistically formative years of the 1930s and 1940s. When examining the cabinet designs used on their games it is noticeable that even in the early 1960s they were using patterns that could easily have come from a 1930s textile design catalogue. Their excellent work was beginning to show its age, and new artists were keen to make changes. Bally employed a freelance artist, Jerry Kelley, who was producing modernist designs like *Capersville* and *Cos-*

mos, while from 1971, Gordon Morison was doing the Gottlieb graphics. Change was under way with styling generally younger, more up to date, and in tune with the rest of the world.

Cabinet artwork also changed at the start of the 1970s. The abstract geometric designs used since the 1930s gave way to cabinet art directly related to the game. Bally's *Eightball* repeated a backglass design of a leather jacketed pool player on the cabinet sides, and Williams' *Liberty Bell*, which celebrated the bicentennial, had the Stars and Stripes prominently stencilled in bright red, white, and blue. Yet besides cabinet artwork development, there were two other reasons why the 1970s was an important decade. The first was the introduction of solid-state electronics into pinball giving the machine a 'brain'. The second reason was infinitely

more important. The earth was about to be invaded . . .

In 1978 the earth was besieged by Atarians, armies of strange blobs descending down a million TV screens. They came not from a galaxy light years away but much nearer home — Japan, land of the rising yen. Their name, Space Invaders. The impact was immediate and universal because here was an arcade game that was totally different. In fact it left pinball behind in the stone age. Space Invaders had all the inter-galactic firepower sights *and* sounds. They were seen and heard everywhere from airport lounges to kebab houses, and they spread like a virus. Invader-zonked-out kids congregated anywhere there was a machine. They developed

SEXY GIRL WAS A 1980 CONVERSION KIT BY THE GERMAN ARKON COMPANY.
HITTING THE G.I.R.L.S. TARGETS LIT UP THE PLAYFIELD SCREEN WITH A PIN-UP GIRL.
THE MORE SKILFUL THE PLAYER, THE NAUGHTIER THE PICTURE.

GOTTLIEB'S *2-player* MAYFAIR

ACTION! FUN! EXCITEMENT!

Swinging target "Double Bonus" scores up to 200 points.

9 rollovers advance red and yellow bonuses.

2 auto-shooters fire ball at swinging target.

4 rollovers turn "pop" bumpers on and off.

Brilliantly illuminated back glass.

Adjustable 3 or 5 ball play.

That Extra Touch of Quality and **ORIGINALITY**

BANNER SPECIALTY COMPANY
1508 - 5th AVENUE
PITTSBURGH 19, PA.

*THIS ATTRACTIVE 1966 GAME, **MAYFAIR**, WAS ROY PARKER'S LAST ARTWORK FOR GOTTLIEB BEFORE RETIRING.*

SPACE INVADERS
516800
00
102
20
00
00
GAME OVE
50
50
50
50
SPACE INVADERS
SPACE INVADERS
SPACE INVADERS

LEFT *THE WARM, SOFT GLOW OF* **SPACE INVADERS** *IN THE DARK GIVES A COMPLETELY DIFFERENT PICTURE TO ITS DAYLIGHT IMAGE.*

ABOVE *IN 1980 BALLY'S BROCHURE CONTAINED A COMIC STRIP STORY OF HOW THE ALIEN MONSTERS ESCAPE FROM THE VIDEO GAMES AND MUTATE INTO THE* **SPACE INVADERS** *PINBALL MACHINE. (PAUL FARIS)*

their own invader-speak. One 12-year-old boy even held up a bank with a shotgun to get coins for the Invader machines, while other schoolkids were allegedly prostituting themselves for Invader cash.

In Japan the little green monsters were gobbling up so many 100 yen pieces that the Japanese mint had to increase production three-fold to keep pace with demand. Clearly something had to be done. In the Philippines, President Marcos completely banned video games. In 1983 Malaysia followed Singapore, Indonesia, and the Philippines banning all public video games following pressure from parents and consumer groups. Authorities in Kuala Lumpur outlawed video games in

*ON GOTTLIEB'S TWO-PLAYER **HI-DOLLY**, ROY PARKER INCORPORATED MANY CHARACTERS FROM HIS PREVIOUS GAMES, FOR EXAMPLE **GAUCHO** AND **SQUARE-HEAD**.*

arcades on the grounds that they glorified violence, destruction, space warfare, and killing.

The pinball boys quickly had to come up with an answer, and they did. If you can't beat 'em—join 'em. In March 1980 Bally attacked planet earth with its *Space Invaders* pinball. Designed by Paul Faris, the backglass had a magnificent alien creature snarling menacingly as if about to attack the player, inspired by the film *Alien* more than the video game. Around the outer edge of the

BALLY'S **BAZAAR**, 1966, HAD A VERY ATTRACTIVE GLASS WITH AN EASTERN
FLAVOUR, THE WORK OF GEORGE MOLENTIN.

ABOVE TWENTY FIVE YEARS AGO BALLY
HIGHLIGHTED THE MAD WORLD WE LIVED IN.
ONE OF ART STENHOLM'S FIRST PIECES FOR
ADVERTISING POSTERS.

IN CONTRAST TO HIS USUAL MODERNIST STYLE, CHRISTIAN MARCHE SHOWED HIS
TALENT FOR COMIC ART ON THIS 1968 BALLY **DIXIELAND**.

backglass were 32 lightbulbs which, by a clever mirror arrangement, were reflected back into infinity producing a three-dimensional effect. There was also a programmed lighting sequence which alternated during play. Bally described it as 'the most exciting pinball game ever produced', a little extravagant with self-praise perhaps, but it was an attractive game and very popular with players. Bally built over 11,000 of this new breed of wide-bodied game, which felt a little strange to play at first. *Space Invaders* had two large 3 inch flippers at the bottom, and two small 2 inch flippers mounted above and to one side of the larger flippers. The surrounding artwork depicted double-barrel death-ray guns pointing and firing towards the playfield targets to heighten the analogy with the video game, backed up by screaming microchip sound effects.

The idea to use alien invaders as a theme was a brilliant marketing success, though the source material was positively ancient. The cinema had used this subject from the earliest days while *The Invaders* was a popular television series during the 1960s. It began memorably with a voiceover saying 'The Invaders . . . alien beings from a dying planet . . . their destination the earth . . . their purpose to make it *their* world.'

Bally brought out a special eight page Space Invaders advertising brochure containing a comic strip story about the inhabitants of a distant planet who needed to invade earth to ensure their own survival. At night armies of the little invaders emerged from the screens of space invader video games. They began to change form and slowly developed into pinball *Space Invaders*. Queues of people formed outside arcades to play the game; a radio commentator is depicted as saying, 'this

unusual phenomenon is baffling experts everywhere – some say it is the hypnotic effect created by the unique, infinity light patterns that is captivating the players of the world. All we know for certain is that Space Invaders pinball with its mysterious appearance is a pinball compulsion never before equalled.' The brochure was good, old-fashioned hype and no doubt helped to make the game very popular.

Bally also fought off the video invaders with its version of *Mr & Mrs Pac-Man* and a few months later with *Baby Pac-Man* (one of the top earning pinballs in 1982). The playfield incorporated a grid of 25 lighted circles, called the pac maze, along which *Pac-Man* travelled, so utilising the elements of video.

What attracted youth to the *Space Invader* video game was the buzz it gave them. Video games were addictive in a way that pinballs never were, and they were far more violent. It was kill or be killed, and the adrenalin flowed. One newspaper reported that a team of research doctors had found some players were even putting their hearts at risk. Dr Douglas Carroll, the psychologist leading the research, said, 'Some video players are undergoing the same stress in play as a managing director trying to control a difficult board meeting; and the heart rate is raised to the level of someone jogging.'

The video invasion continued throughout the early 1980s. After Space Invaders came a host of similar aliens doing their syncopated war shuffle across the video screen for the benefit of the battle scarred, glazed-eyed video freak. Through the cosmos via the interstellar microchips came the *Galaxians*, *Asteroids*, *Defenders*, *Cosmic Aliens* and *Pleiads*. There was even a video called *Gorf*, presumably named after the indestructible robot in the cult 1950s sci-fi film *The Day the Earth Stood Still* starring Michael Rennie. (Older cinema-goers will remember how Michael Rennie left instructions for Gorf with his dying breath – 'Gorf . . . Klaatu, barodnee Nikto.' No-one ever knew what it meant but it became the cult phrase of the time. It roughly translated as 'Gorf, one day they'll name a video game after you!')

Other video games were based on lunar landings. There were no screaming blasting laser guns, only the aim to set the lunar lander safely and sedately on the moon. In contrast, *Turbo* involved sitting in your own racing-car video cockpit and driving at maniacal speed over an ever-changing terrain. *Frogger* meant you were a little green frog trying to cross the road without getting splatted! For the insectivorous there was *Centipede* in which a wriggly insect comes towards you. If

Enter the Vectordome and Play

Guided by the PAC, Play Analysis Computer voice, you are ready to plan your Vector game attack. The ball is your Vector energy beam and the Vectorscan ramp is the goal.

Enter Vector's bi-level field through the unique figure-8 skill shot and start your play. Gain entry to the Vectorscan ramp and measure the speed of your flip-shot, which is then displayed on the center playfield's digital "Flip-O-Meter" readout. For further challenge, the Flip-O-Meter also shows the fastest flip-to-date. Vectorscan flip speed is converted to points, and beating the fastest flip-to-date will award a Special. Your Vectorscan bonus score is also displayed on the Flip-O-Meter when the Bonus Light is on.

To gain entry to the Vectorscan ramp, it is nec-essary to drop the Defender drop targets that guard the ramp. Shooting Defenders 1-3 in sequence qualifies the top saucers for up to 3 captured balls, or Vector energy units. When Defenders 1-3 are knocked down out of sequence, Defenders 4-6 must also be hit to qualify top saucers for captured balls.

...ng the upper level X-Y-Z drop targets in sequence will drop ...orscan Defender targets, one at a time, by remote control.

...s bottom playfield sports 2 new bottom saucers for last chance Save-A-... maximize your Vector game play.

...ppers provide maximum ball control for multiple skill shots.

Bally's Game of the Future

Captured ball Energy Units can be released 3 ways: By capturing all 3 balls, by making the H-Y-P-E targets in sequence, or by a unique last ball feature. On the last ball only the H-Y-P-E targets may be hit out of order, releasing one captured ball. Vector's Equitable Multi-Ball has memory and recall for each player's ultra-scoring possibilities.

Vector's exciting graphic pack-age includes a multi-plane back-glass with infinity lighting that brings the Vectordome's field to life.

you zapped him he divided and grew a new head. Every game was a winner.

One pinball enthusiast nostalgically remarked, 'To me, pinball has had it commercially. It epitomises a time gone by, a time of gaudy cabinets, comic art back-flashes, and buzzing relays, but above all, a good laugh. The video age is here now, clean, sterile, boring and lacklustre. Pinball machines have become like your favourite record collection, kept at home, played with your mates, and full of old memories.' But he was wrong. Pinball had a future, though it was certainly going through a bad patch. Partly this was down to the competition, partly perhaps because pinball operators were sometimes giving their customers just three balls

per game. The east coast of America was known as three-ball country (whereas the west coast played with five balls), prompting one trade newspaper to remark: 'How can the operator expect to create an interest in pinball by getting only three balls? With today's flipper games being much faster and more complicated than the older electro-mechanical games, three balls can drain out of play in the time taken by the pre-game set-up on *Donkey Kong*.'

PROMOTION-HUNGRY ROCK GROUP 'KISS' APPROACHED BALLY TO BRING OUT THIS CLASSIC GAME. STYLISH ARTWORK FROM KEVIN O'CONNOR.

Eventually, however, the video market reached saturation point, and pinball began to revive. One amusement operator in South Carolina recalled, 'Quite by accident in the winter of 1981 and 1982 when every location was lined with wall-to-wall videos, we put in a couple of old flippers as fillers. To our surprise in many cases the $300 dollar flipper was taking as much money as the $2,700 video game.' The writing was on the wall. And the pinball manufacturers were introducing a few secret weapons of their own. The same technology that had put video games out in front was now being used against them. Electronic sound effects and voice synthesisers were introduced into pinball. In

his book *Invasion of the Space Invaders* Martin Amis recounts how, when hungover one New Year's Day in 1980, he entered a bar with a friend near the Pantheon in Paris, and ordered a coffee and croissants. Suddenly the silence was shattered by an unearthly disembodied guttural voice proclaiming, 'Heed Gorgar! Heed! Gorgar speaks!' His friend, who had drunk a considerable amount of calvados, thought the voice emanated from a pinball machine and staggered away from the bar exclaiming, 'I can't cope with that!'

They had, in fact, encountered pinball's new secret weapon. *Gorgar*, made by Williams in late 1979, was the first talking pinball, and had a number of phrases

such as 'You beat me' and 'Gorgar hurt'. In the background a heartbeat noise increases in speed and intensity as the game progresses, whipping up a similar response in the player. It made the adrenalin flow in the same way that video games did.

Although *Gorgar* was not an outstanding game, the artwork by Constantino Mitchell was extremely attractive. On the backglass Gorgar was depicted as a green-eyed red-devil monster. In front of Gorgar was a superhero rescuing a scantily clad, beautiful maiden from his clutches. Gorgar was also screened across the middle of the playfield where there were sundry artwork effects including the serpent monster emanating

BANZAI RUN WAS A UNIQUE GAME THAT CONTINUED THE PLAYFIELD ACTION INTO THE BACKBOX. (MARK SPRENGER)

from a corner of the playfield called the pit. The cabinet was stencilled with a flame effect and the word 'Gorgar' in large letters, producing one of the most attractive machines ever made. In many ways the graphics were reminiscent of the artwork on Bally's Fireball eight years earlier.

The idea of a talking pintable was nothing new — it had been envisaged as long ago as 1935. In *Automatic*

World magazine one writer suggested: 'All you have to do is to link up a gramophone with the various score points and provide a record which will maintain a running commentary on the quality of play saying: 'rotten shot', 'serves you right for using duds', 'what d'you expect for a penny?', 'stop tilting the table you mutt', 'scoot for your life, here comes a detective – this is a pay-out joint'. 'I'm telling you – talkie tables are bound to come!!' Fifty-four years later this prophet's words became a reality!

Williams quickly followed this up with another success, *Firepower*. The latter trespassed on video territory by using artwork depicting a modern fighter aircraft dealing out multi-directional instant annihilation from its arsenal of weapons, a scenario proffered by 90 per cent of successful video games. The games war was well and truly on. This was the first electronic machine to feature multi-ball, whereby a player could hit the *Firepower* targets and have three balls in play simultaneously. Multi-ball had a similar play appeal to video-games because the player had to concentrate on several moving objects at once demanding complete concen-

tration to avoid losing a ball. *Firepower* also had a feature called lane change. The illuminated lanes at the top of the playfield could be altered by pressing the flipper buttons, and quick reaction was needed to alter the lane lights as the ball headed for the different paths.

Firepower, the most popular machine of 1980, was designed by Steve Ritchie, one of the best pinball designers in the world. His employer, the Williams Manufacturing Company needed to keep up the pressure against the space invaders, and so gave Ritchie *carte blanche* to go ahead with his next brainchild. The result – pinball with two-level playfields, each with its own flippers and joined by ramps up which the ball could be propelled. It was a gamble, and Williams were worried about the cost and complexity of such a machine but the company realised that something drastic had to be done. The ramps had to be designed so that the ball would smoothly run up and down

PENCIL ROUGH FOR A PROPOSED DATA EAST GAME BASED ON THE EDGAR WALLACE STORY KING KONG, A GIANT APE WHICH TERRORISED NEW YORK. (KEVIN O'CONNOR)

KEVIN O'CONNOR'S ORIGINAL ARTWORK FOR DATA EAST'S **KING KONG**. THE GAME NEVER WENT INTO PRODUCTION.

PINBALL ART

PREVIOUS PAGE *TONY RAMUNNI*
PAINTED THE ARRESTING BACKGLASS
FOR WILLIAMS' **BLACK KNIGHT** *IN 1980.*

KEVIN O'CONNOR HOLDING THE ORIGINAL **KISS** *ARTWORK.*

ARTIST MARGARET HUDSON WITH TWO OF HER PINBALL ARTWORKS: THE ORIGINAL
PAC-MAN *GRAPHICS AND* **THE SIMPSONS** *PLAYFIELD BASED ON THE SUCCESSFUL*
AMERICAN TV CARTOON SERIES.

without 'chatter' or 'clatter'. The prototype machine was built full-size on a 'bread board' (with no artwork or decoration). Drop targets and one powered bumper were added, and the various features and targets were shuffled around until the machine worked perfectly without any dead spots. All that was left was a theme. 'I always wanted one involving knights', said Ritchie, so the name *Black Knight* was chosen. 'I like the idea of macho themes, and so do the kids, and your average pinball player is a 15-year-old boy. The pinball machine is great for taking out your violent and aggressive fantasies.'

Black Knight also had speech, the phrases being digitally recorded and then slowed down. Amusingly, the weak 'S' sound in the word 'slay' had to be emphasised to avoid any embarrassing misunderstanding by female players when the machine proclaimed 'Black Knight will slay you!' This was a problem that had occurred on a prototype of Bally's *Kiss* the previous year! When *Black Knight* was unveiled at the Amusement and Music Operators of America (AMOA) exhibition in Chicago, the showcase for 150 new video and pinball games, it caused a sensation. Many of the video games such as *Defender*, *Pac-Man*, and *Battlezone* later

became household names, but it was *Black Knight* they found themselves queueing to play. Ralph Lally, editor of the amusement trade paper *Play Meter*, watched the three balls zapping round *Black Knight's* two levels in awe and remarked, 'this will make every previous pinball game obsolete.' One arcade owner who had completely gone over to videos came back to pinball with a *Black Knight*. And the first machine on location in Chicago took over $500 in one week, more than any other pinball or video in the arcade.

Although by 1982 the video bubble had peaked and burst, things were still tough on the pinball front. With manufacturers having to cut costs pinball went back to basics, cutting down on unnecessary expense by revamping older designs. Sometimes electronic versions of the best electro-mechanicals were released as in *Fireball II* and *El Dorado* based on the 1970s original designs. Game Plan brought out *Sharpshooter II*, an updated version of the game designed by pinball author

*A ONE-EYED SKULL ON TOP OF THE BACK BOX WAS ALL PART OF THE SPOOKY FUN ON GOTTLIEB'S 1989 **BONE BUSTER**.*

FOXY LADY WAS A FOUR-PLAYER COCKTAIL TABLE MACHINE MADE BY GAME PLAN, STYLED FOR THE MORE SOPHISTICATED LOCATION.

Roger Sharpe, this time with the added pleasure of gunfire, rattlesnake, and exploding dynamite sound effects. George Molentin had worked on the artwork for the original *Sharpshooter*, one of the last before he retired.

Meanwhile, the steel ball rolled on. In 1984 Williams brought out a popular game, *Space Shuttle*, which combined the hit ingredients of a great game and great artwork. With pinball prices going ever upwards the amusement operator had to be certain that he bought only the best money-spinners. And with *Space Shuttle* he was safe. The voice, which was missing from several of Williams' previous games as an economy measure, was back. Mission Control talked the player through the game, and there was an attractive 3-D model of the space shuttle featured on the playfield.

The same year, sadly, one of the big manufacturers, Stern Electronics, decided to close down its pinball division. It had been in existence since 1976, and under the name Chicago Coin since the 1930s. In 1985 came another closure, with Game Plan finishing its operation. In Italy, in contrast the pinball manufacturer Zaccaria had not been standing still. Its latest machines were feature packed. *Farfalla*, *Magic Castle*, and *Devil Riders*

all had the innovative ingredient whereby the player had to complete a sequence which lowered a ball ramp allowing access to the upper playfield. *Farfalla* had very attractive artwork depicting a diaphanously dressed lady butterfly in gossamer drapes, while the female voice emanating from the machine said, 'I like playing with you!' The Italian manufacturers were probably blissfully unaware of the double-entendre. No matter. No hot-blooded American could resist it.

'Farfalla' is the Italian word for butterfly and it was the only Italian game not to have its title translated into English. On the other hand when titles were translated this was not always done too successfully. Zaccaria's *Wood's Queen* depicted a female Tarzan on the backglass swinging on a vine, surrounded by wild animals. A more apt title would have been *Jungle Queen* – you do not get many lions and elephants in a wood!

By 1986 pinball had become virtually unrecognisable from the game of just a few years before, the gameplans having become so sophisticated and fast. Ramps and chrome wireform tubes proliferated across the playfield. One pinball enthusiast who had bought the original 1980 Williams' *Black Knight* for home use had to sell it after playing the 1989 version *Black Knight* 2000. He just could not go back to the nine-year-old game, even though it had been a showstopper in its time. By 1990 all the manufacturers were bringing out stupendous machines, and they never looked back. Amusement operators gradually started giving more and more space back to the pinball, a trend which is still continuing. The Phoenix had risen from the ashes.

CHAPTER 4

THE WORLD OF THE PINBALL ARTIST

'AROUND 1950 LYN DURANT, A WELL-KNOWN CHARACTER IN THE INDUSTRY, WENT TO HIS PINBALL CABINET MAKER IN WISCONSIN TAKING WITH HIM ADVERTISING POSTERS' ARTIST JOE MACHIK TO HELP SELECT THE COLORS FOR THE CABINET. DURANT LOOKED AT JOE, AND JOE HAD ON A BEAUTIFUL SILK TIE: IT COST ABOUT $40 EVEN IN THOSE DAYS. THAT WAS A VERY EXPENSIVE TIE, AND DURANT TOOK A PAIR OF SCISSORS AND CLIPPED HIS TIE OFF AND HANDED IT TO THE CABINET SHOP AND TOLD THEM THAT WAS THE COLOR HE WANTED THE CABINET!'

WENDELL McADAMS (FORMER PRESIDENT OF GAME PLAN).

Pinball art is not the art of Rembrandt or Turner, and it is not the pop art of Warhol or Hockney. Nor is it the comic art of Lichtenstein or the cubism of Braque or Picasso. Yet it has borrowed ingredients from all of them. It is a melting pot of many different styles and subjects painted by many different artists, combining movie poster art, comic-book art, the British saucy seaside postcard with a touch of Norman Rockwell.

Of the many different kinds of artists the pinball artist has remained one of the most anonymous, and until recent times he was not even allowed to sign his work. Yet the fact remains these people are by the very nature of their work some of the most talented and versatile artists working today. It is only when their talents are turned towards 'easel art', paintings designed to be hung in the home and galleries, that they tend to achieve recognition and acclaim. But things are changing; original pinball artwork as well as the printed glasses are now eagerly collected. It is also worth pointing out that fringe art has been an excellent training ground for many. Sir Alfred Munnings, who became president of the British Royal Academy of Art at the age of 23, served his apprenticeship in advertising. And the first creations of many people – such as an acetate of Mickey Mouse drawn by Walt Disney – are now expensive, period-piece collector's items.

One of the most respected artists in the history of pinball was Leroy (Roy) Parker. In his early days, before World War II, he had been employed as a truck signwriter, a craft that requires a high degree of skill, precision and versatility. He then joined independent printers the Reproduction Company in the 1930's. Reproduction, owned by the Usedom family, handled all of Gottlieb's work and during his years there Parker did the artwork for literally hundreds of pinball machines. (The artist is not only responsible for the glass and playfield, but also the plastic lightshields and the cabinet artwork which is applied using simple stencils.)

Parker's work was best characterised by his humorous glasses. In fact you could look at a Parker backglass and find all kinds of amusing incidental details in odd corners. He also knew how to draw an attractive female. But despite the undoubted pressure of coming up with something new every month, Parker never lowered his standards, and some of his last work is his finest. The designs for most of the games that Parker painted were the work of Wayne Neyens, and together this formidable team made a fortune for Gottlieb. Wayne recalls:

Roy Parker had a dry sense of humor which comes over in his work. Sometimes he'd say something with a straight face and you didn't know if he was joking or not. He had a little studio at home and sometimes he'd come over to our place late afternoon, we'd tell him what we wanted and he'd go home and work on it half the night, maybe all night sometimes, and he'd be there in the morning with a sketch, waiting for us to come in! We'd start out with a theme in mind, I'd perhaps draw a rough picture, put them on a backbox to see what it looked like and Parker would come in and pick up the theme and make a drawing out of my mess. He had a fairly free hand.

DR. DAVID BANNER GETTING ANGRY ON THE
BACKGLASS OF THE **INCREDIBLE HULK** (1979).
(GORDON MORISON)

LEFT *GORDON MORISON'S ORIGINAL PENCIL DRAWING FOR GOTTLIEB'S **INCREDIBLE
HULK**.*

Neyens and Parker produced many classic games such as *Criss Cross*, *World Fair*, *Majorettes*, *Slick Chick*, and *Gigi*. Sadly, Parker fell ill around 1966 and died shortly afterwards. His last artwork for Gottlieb was *Mayfair*, released in June 1966. Before Parker died he worked for another company specialising in pinball art, Advertising Posters, which now handled all Williams, Bally, and Chicago Coin's work. Advertising Posters was formed in 1932 by Thomas Grant (an advertising artist), and John van Ansdale (a pinball engineer). George Molentin had done their artwork since 1935 on a freelance basis, working on the Williams, Exhibit, Bally,

MOULIN ROUGE FEATURED AN ARTIST HOLDING A SKETCH PAD WHICH PROGRESSIVELY LIGHTS UP TO REVEAL A PAINTING OF THE FAMOUS PARISIAN NIGHT CLUB. (ART STENHOLM)

United and later, Midway Games. He became Art Director in 1961, supervising about five other artists there. The company was now doing the artwork for 99 per cent of the pinball machines produced in the world. The reason for the move was that in the late 1950s, Reproduction had a couple of serious fires which destroyed all their screens and equipment, so the

*THE BEAUTIFUL **NORTH STAR** WAS ART STENHOLM'S FIRST WORK FOR GOTTLIEB IN 1964. HE HAD THE UNENVIABLE TASK OF CONTINUING THE TRADITIONAL GOTTLIEB STYLE DEVELOPED BY ROY PARKER.*

Gottlieb contract (including Parker) went over to Advertising Posters.

From the mid-1960s Parker's replacement was Art Stenholm who worked mainly on the Gottlieb contract, having previously been involved on the classic Williams' Heatwave (1964) and Eager Beaver (1965). His work was similar to Parker's, and in fact the very first game

he painted for Gottlieb was *North Star* in 1964 which is often mistakenly credited to his predecessor.

In 1970 Gordon Morison took over the Gottlieb job at Advertising Posters, creating the artwork on hundreds of pinball games. Like most of the artists working in pinball Morison displayed a talent from an early age: when other kids were reading comics he was creating his own. One of Morison's many anecdotes from his early days goes as follows: 'One of our artists, Chris Marche, spent three days on a magnificent color layout for a game called *Speedshift*, a neat bit of work that was admired by a lot of people including George Molentin. It

ARTIST CHRISTIAN MARCHE ILLUSTRATED SCORES OF GAMES FOR WILLIAMS AND BALLY DURING THE 1960S AND 1970S.

wasn't until it was being shown to the client that it was noticed that the beautiful lettering spelt out *Speedshit*! Proof that when you letter you can't spell, and when you spell you can't letter.'

Morison was one of the first to break away from the traditional geometric designs on cabinet artwork: 'The cabinet designs were all stencilled so they had to be kept simple. If you started to get into illustrations it made it really hard for the stencillers. When I once visited them they begged me not to do complicated designs . . . it was driving them out of their minds!'

Frenchman Christian Marche shared an office with Morison having started working at the company in 1964. He worked mainly on the Williams' games for the next 14 years or so, while also tackling some for

Bally and Chicago Coin. Marche had a diversity of styles which enabled him to do cartoon characters, as in the attractive Bally *Dixieland* and an offbeat, spiky, contemporary style which he used on a great number of games such as *Op-Pop-Pop*, *Zodiac*, and *Miss O*. Marche describes the story behind *Miss O:* 'I originally called the game *Miss Q*, a play on the word 'mis-cue', as one of the pool players was mis-cueing the ball. The glass showed a group of teenagers playing pool. In the foreground a young girl with a shapely bottom was

ORIGINAL PENCIL DRAWING AND COLOUR SKETCH FOR WILLIAMS' *SUPERSTAR* (1972) FROM THE ERA OF THE BEAT GROUPS. (CHRISTIAN MARCHE)

leaning over the pool table with her cue. Unfortunately I had forgotten that the French word for backside is *cul* which is pronounced the same as the letter 'Q'. At the last minute, to my horror, I realised that *Miss Q* in France would sound like 'Miss Backside'! That is why it was hastily altered from a 'Q' to an 'O' and ended up with the curious title *Miss O!*'

In 1965 Williams used the freelance artist Jerry Kelley to create the artwork on a game called *Pot O' Gold*. This was the first machine to break away from the traditional style and use a modernist, semi-abstract approach. Kelley then worked on several machines for Bally over the next few years. He had a distinctive, angular contemporary style that was a little different to the usual artwork, which the public liked. His work appears on the very successful *Capersville*, *Dogies*, and *Cosmos*, amongst others. His views on pinball artwork are as sharp as his style: 'When I came into pinball my style was way ahead of anything around at the time and there was a lot of resistance to change. I had to convince them that my style was the art of the future. One boss at Williams wanted red, white, and blue in every game. I never used those colors on any of my games. I also used a lot of black but they said "That represents disaster – we don't want any of that " – but it was just a new way of doing the thing. For instance all the other pinball artists were drawing buxom girls whereas mine had a modern look. My first game for Bally was *Capersville* which came out in 1966. It sold a record number, over 5,000 (their previous production runs had been in the region of 600–800). They got really excited, but it had been an uphill struggle for me; they had even argued that the name *Capersville* wasn't a proper name and didn't make sense.'

Kelley had originally designed a revolutionary style one-armed bandit slot machine for Bally early in the 1960s. Again he had met with opposition but the new machine went into production and was so successful that nearly all the other slot manufacturers went bankrupt. (This wasn't the first time that Bally had put the competition out of business. Back in 1937 its new game *Bumper* used the first spring-style electric scoring bumpers and illuminated rotating scoring disc and had been so successful that many opponents went to the wall.)

Kelley's replacement from 1968–77 was Dick White, who worked on *4 Million BC* and *Nip-It*, amongst other popular games. In 1971 David Christensen was also at Bally, working in the engineering department drawing up service manuals. As a sideline experiment he thought

ABOVE *WILLIAMS'* **SUPERSTAR** *PROMOTIONAL BROCHURE.*

ABOVE RIGHT *WILLIAMS'* **MISS O** *USED THE ANGULAR STYLING THAT WAS POPULAR AROUND 1970. (CHRISTIAN MARCHE)*

RIGHT *BALLY'S* **NIP-IT** *FEATURED A CROCODILE BALL-GRABBER UNIT ON THE PLAYFIELD. THIS ARTWORK WAS BY BALLY'S IN-HOUSE ARTIST DICK WHITE IN 1973.*

BELOW BALLY'S **AIR ACES** ORIGINALLY SHOWED AEROPLANES SINKING A BATTLESHIP AND LED TO ARTIST DAVE CHRISTENSEN BEING ACCUSED OF HAVING A WARLIKE MENTALITY.

Bally AIR ACES

4-PLAYER FLIPPER-TYPE PINBALL

CONVERTIBLE TO ADD-A-BALL

DOUBLE SPECIAL LANES

EXTRA BALLS KICKOUT HOLE

New DROP TARGETS

UPPER DECK FLIPPERS

20,000 TO

DOUBL

1, 2, 3 OR ★ **4** ★ CAN PLAY

he would design a pinball glass. He called it *Fireball* and the rest, as they say, is history! Dave recalls those days: '*Fireball* was basically inspired by a comic-book character with the same name. He had a body swathed in flame and was one of a trio of comic-book characters who went round solving crimes. I knew nothing about pinball artwork so I made it up at home using clear films, cut out in a basic way. I showed it to Bally and it

went into production.' Released in February 1972 it sold over 3,800 units, well above average. Since then, *Fireball* has become a legend and is now something of a collector's item.

The outstanding point about Christensen's art was that it leapt from the traditional cosy look into the space-age. He was a rebel who was not interested in corny cartoon characters and wanted to push back the barriers. Roy Parker's girls may have had curves but Christensen's had curves with a capital 'C'. Needless to say he had his share of clashes with the Bally management. 'I started sneaking in a little shadow area where the nipple was, then Paul Faris and Kevin O'Connor were putting them in too. In *Air Aces* (which I did for Bally in 1975) the fleet of aeroplanes in the background was originally diving down and destroying a battleship, but because of the disgust at the time over Vietnam I was accused of having a warlike mentality, so I had to get rid of the battleship. Now there's this poor goof on the backglass standing there saying "mission accomplished". Nobody knew exactly what he meant but the whole idea was that they'd destroyed a battleship.'

BELOW *CAPERSVILLE WAS BALLY'S FIRST GAME USING JERRY K. KELLEY'S MODERNIST ARTWORK IN 1966. CAPERSVILLE SOLD OVER 5000 GAMES, A PRODUCTION RECORD AT THE TIME.*

ABOVE *BALLY'S CAPTAIN FANTASTIC IS A CLASSIC EXAMPLE OF ANATOMICALLY IMPOSSIBLE FEMALE PULCHRITUDE, BY DAVE CHRISTENSEN.*

Christensen sneaked another dubious touch into *Captain Fantastic*. The *Tommy* inspired machine had a crowd scene in the background including a curvaceous young lady with her hand behind her back. The guy standing directly behind has a startled expression on his face! 'She was grabbing the guy in retaliation', he explained. 'They put a silver star over it when it was discovered, but some slipped through at first.' During Christensen's 10 years at Bally he undoubtedly created some of the finest artwork ever seen on a pinball machine. His *Fireball*, *Captain Fantastic*, *Wizard*, and *Nitro Groundshaker* are now all considered classics. (Incidentally on *Nitro Groundshaker* he pictured himself behind the wheel of one of the cars on the playfield. Another figure in the picture is an Indianapolis racing

RIGHT *FUTURISTIC STYLING BY TONY RAMUNNI ON THIS RECENT PINBALL FROM THE ITALIAN COMPANY MR. GAME.*
BELOW
FIREBALL II *WAS DAVE CHRISTENSEN'S LAST ARTWORK FOR BALLY.*

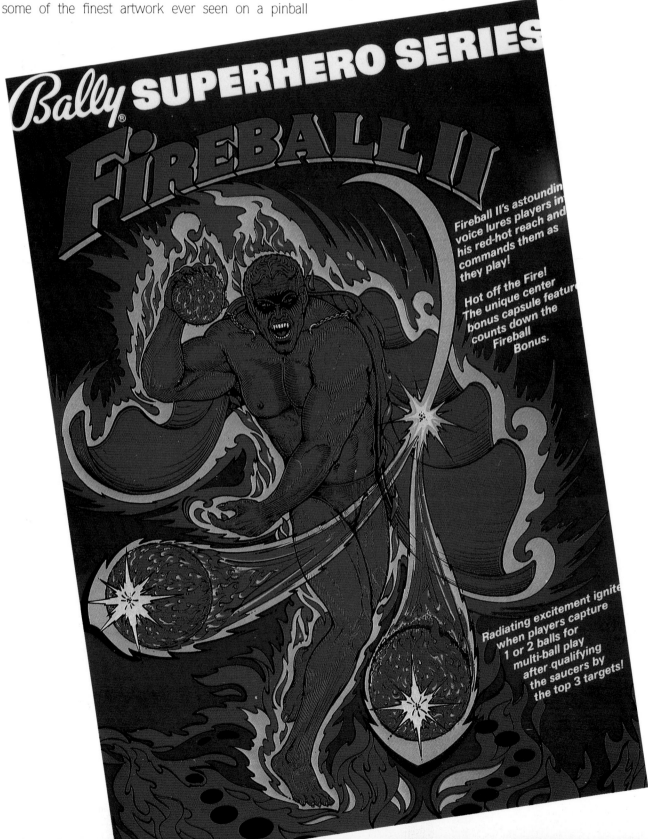

driver who became a friend. And pinball veteran Norm Clark is portrayed as a mechanic.) One of the distinguishing features of Christensen's work is the unusual belt buckles. This interest started from a friend in the belt buckle business for whom he designed novelty buckles for as a sideline. One unusual set of designs was based on slot machines — they went into production in the 1970s.

Around 1980, with competition from video games, pinball was having a hard time. However Williams received a boost with good sales of *Black Knight*, the

first two-level game with ramps. Designer Steve Ritchie chose the Black Knight theme for the game. It was based on Sir Percy of Scandia, a knight of the round table in King Arthur's sixth-century Camelot. Sir Percy

*THE **EIGHT BALL DELUXE** ARTWORK IS BY THAT RARE PHENOMENON A WOMAN PINBALL ARTIST: MARGARET HUDSON USED A FAMILY FRIEND TO MODEL AS THE POOL PLAYER.*

adopted the black knight disguise to serve his king both as the unassuming member of the royal court and as the mysterious avenging champion.

Tony Ramunni did the graphics on *Black Knight*. He emigrated to America from Italy when he was 15. While still at school he took a job at Williams helping in the engineering department, and one day did a quick sketch of his boss. Tony recalls, 'Before you knew it I was doing 15-minute sketches of the whole company. Steve Kordek discovered me and transferred me to the art department.' Having worked at various times on games for Bally and Williams, he was tempted back to Italy by an offer from Marino Zaccaria, and working for Mr Game in Bologna, producing futuristic looking pinballs such as *Dakar, World Cup '90,* and *Mac Attack.*

Despite the success of *Black Knight* the industry as a whole was having problems. In 1982 Stern Electronics finished with pinball, as did Game Plan in 1985. There was a similar picture in Europe with the major manufacturer, Zaccaria, eventually closing in Italy. In America Bally was in trouble and its amusement games division was eventually taken over by Williams Electronics in 1988. As one manager at Williams remarked, 'Two dogs can ruin a company — Bally had a whole kennelful!' Still, there was some good news. A new pinball

A NICE PIECE OF ARTWORK FROM PAUL FARIS. **ANDROMEDA** *WAS MADE BY THE NOW DEFUNCT GAME PLAN COMPANY.*

manufacturer Data East, had sprung up in Chicago with Paul Faris as its chief artist. Faris originally joined Bally in the 1970s working alongside David Christensen, his first games for the company being *Night Rider, Lost World, Playboy,* and the best post-war seller, the original *Eight Ball* (the first game to sell over 20,000). In 1980 Faris did the artwork for the *Space Invaders* pinball which had a striking backglass depicting a hideous alien monster. What was different about it was the clever use of a special reflective glass which gave an 'infinity' lighting effect. All the lights, titles and scores in the backbox were reflected further and further back into the distance.

Faris was also responsible for setting up Bally's in-house screen printing department in the 1970s, and

PREVIOUS PAGE *IN 1990 BRITAIN'S FIRST SATELLITE TV STATION, SKY, COMMISSIONED STEPHEN MAY TO DESIGN A SPECIAL PINBALL GLASS TO USE ON THEIR TOP 40 POP MUSIC PROGRAMME.*

BELOW *DATA EAST CLOSED OFF A WHOLE STREET FOR THIS MOVIE-STYLE SET TO SHOOT THE PHOTOGRAPHIC BACKGLASS FOR* **SECRET SERVICE** *IN 1987.*

ABOVE *MAGIC MARKER SKETCH FOR BALLY'S **STAR TREK**. THESE UNIFORMS ARE FROM THE TELEVISION SERIES BUT WERE LATER CHANGED TO COLOURS USED IN THE FILM. (KEVIN O'CONNOR)*

RIGHT *BALLY'S **STAR TREK** SHOWING THE REVISED UNIFORMS AS WORN IN THE MOTION PICTURE.*

he developed the four-colour process which has now partially replaced the older screen printing methods. Bally's *Lost World* was the first four-colour instance of a painting being used for the artwork and thus being photographically reproduced. (Before *Lost World* all glasses were produced using black line art and solid colour separations. Every colour that was printed required a separate screen.) In the late 1980s Williams and Bally made great strides in pinball design and left the competition far behind. Steve Ritchie has been described as 'probably the best pinball designer in the world', and his talents and those of his brother Mark, and other top-notch game designers including Barry Oursler and Denis Nordman, combined with the brilliant graphics of the best ever team of artists in the business – Python Anghelo, John Youssi, Pat McMahon, Mark Sprenger, Doug Watson and Greg Freres, have given us superb, fast and exciting games – *F. 14 Tomcat*, *Black Knight 2000*, *Whirlwind*, *Banzai Run*, *Police Force*, *Elvira*, and *Rollergames* – all packed with features.

LEFT *DATA EAST'S PROMOTIONAL BROCHURE FOR PLAYBOY MIMICKED THE CENTRE SPREAD FROM THE MAGAZINE.*

Doug Watson originally worked at Advertising Posters with Gordon Morison in the early 1980s, and two striking examples of his work are Williams' *Barracora* (1981) and Gottlieb's *Devils Dare* (1982). Greg Freres is the head of the Williams art department. He originally worked in advertising until Kevin O'Connor called him to say that Bally were looking for new artists. Games he has done for Bally include *Harlem Globetrotters*, *Fathom* and *Elvira*.

Unfortunately, this has not been a complete list of all the artists who ever worked in pinball, but at least it has brought some very talented artists out of the anonymity of the days when they were even forbidden to sign their names on their own work. Today, however, the entire creative design team is usually credited on the machine itself, and the roles of game designer and artist are much closer than they once were.

*BELOW THE SKETCH FOR DATA EAST'S **PLAYBOY** UPON WHICH THE FINAL DESIGN WAS BASED. (KEVIN O'CONNOR)*

*LEFT REJECTED BACKGLASS DESIGN FOR DATA EAST'S 1989 **PLAYBOY**. (KEVIN O'CONNOR)*

BELOW *THE PHOTOGRAPHIC BACKGLASS OF* **PLAYBOY** *TO CELEBRATE THEIR 35TH ANNIVERSARY. HUGH HEFNER IS WITH HIS FUTURE WIFE, PLAYMATE KIMBERLEY CONRAD. ARTIST KEVIN O'CONNOR IS IN THE BACKGROUND WEARING A BLUE SHIRT.*

ABOVE *THE ORIGINAL 1978* **PLAYBOY** *FEATURED SOME OF PAUL FARIS' FIRST ARTWORK FOR BALLY.*

CHAPTER 5

THE PINBALL HALL OF FAME

If there is one thing that people need to rescue them from the grip of a depression, as they did in the 1930s, to boost their morale and raise their spirits, it is a superhero, even a fictional one. Top of the list, at various times, have been Flash Gordon, Spiderman, and Superman. And their reward — star billing on pinball machines!

Flash Gordon originally appeared as a newspaper cartoon strip by Alex Raymond in the 1930s, and then

in 1936 as a Universal Films weekly cinema serial starring Buster Crabbe. With his female companion, Dale Arden, he set off in Dr Zarkov's rocket ship to thwart Emperor Ming of the planet Mongo. (OK, you've read the comic and seen the film, now play the pinball.) Bally brought out *Flash Gordon* in 1981, hot on the

BELOW *KEVIN O'CONNOR'S ORIGINAL ARTWORK FOR THE BACKGLASS OF BALLY'S 1981* **FLASH GORDON**.

RIGHT *THE NAME OF GORDON MORISON'S GIRLFRIEND, SUE, IS HIDDEN ON PRINCESS ARDALA'S BIKINI TOP.*

heels of Williams' *Black Knight*. The latter was the first pinball to have a second level on the playfield onto which the ball could be flipped by skilful shots up metal ramps. *Flash Gordon* had a very similar arrangement, the upper level being called 'Ming's palace', named after the dreaded Emperor Ming. Painted by Kevin O'Connor, the game had a very attractive, predominantly red backglass with Flash Gordon wielding a mighty sword, Dale Arden behind him, and the Emperor Ming below. What was most striking about the glass though was Bally's use of a blindingly bright stroboscopic light between the words 'Flash' and 'Gordon'.

In the annals of comic book history there evolved a plethora of supercharacters, each endowed with the kind of powers you wished you possessed when your car was bumped off the road by a juggernaut. There has even been a Super Ted, the world's most remarkable teddy bear who could spread his paws and fly like an aeroplane. (Flying seems to come easy to superheroes!) Then there was Superwitch, Supermum, Superdad, and Supergirl. The Super Seven was a group of kids from the *Knockout* comic who nobly pursued justice for schoolkids everywhere.

But these characters are mere underlings in the company of the grand-daddy of them all, Superman, who made his first appearance in a comic in June 1938, the sole survivor of the exploding planet Krypton. Rocketed to earth as a baby, Kal-El grew to manhood with superpowers bestowed on him by the yellow sun and lighter gravity. Superman's alter-ego was bumbling Clark Kent, a reporter on the *Daily Planet* who when danger threatened found a convenient telephone kiosk to drop his pants and remove his glasses as he metamorphosed into the saviour of the world. Such questions as 'Why did Lois Lane never see through his thin disguise of one pair of black spectacles?' or 'Did anyone ever hand in Clark Kent's clothes at the police station?' were never asked of superheroes!

Created by Jerry Siegel and Joe Shuster, Superman was hugely successful. He made his first appearance on

BELOW *EVEL KNIEVEL WAS A BIG STAR IN 1977 WHEN BALLY RELEASED THE PINBALL BEARING HIS NAME. (PAUL FARIS)*

LEFT *IN 1975 DAVE CHRISTENSEN PRODUCED THIS STUNNING ARTWORK FOR BALLY'S **WIZARD** WHICH WAS LAUNCHED IN THE WAKE OF THE MOVIE TOMMY.*

celluloid in 1953, the title role being played by George Reeves. Then, after a gap of 25 years, he reappeared on film in 1978 with near-namesake Christopher Reeve in the title role, surely everyone's idea of what Superman should look like. Reeve won the part after 200 hopefuls had been rejected. The *Superman* movie eventually increased to *Superman II, III,* and *IV,* but by 1979 Krypton Man had been immortalised by the pinball manufacturer Atari with its wide-bodied game called, quite simply, Superman. Atari was already a leading name in video games when it produced its first pinball *The Atarians* in 1977. Superman was its last and most successful game before it finally retreated from pinball manufacturing. Not even Superman could help them!

Another unlikely superhero arrived in the shape of Spiderman – always prefixed with 'Amazing'. His alter-ego was Peter Parker, a shy teenage bookworm. When he was bitten by a radioactive spider, a misfortune that would have despatched most of us to the mortuary, Peter found himself possessed of all the arachnid's powers: spinning webs, hanging from ceilings, and climbing walls. Spiderman was a comparative new-comer to the world of comic superheroes. He first appeared in *Pow* in 1967, drawn by Steve Ditko, and made his pinball debut in 1980 with Gottlieb. The pinball backglass was very striking, which is usually the case when the central character is bright red, as with Fireball and Gorgar. This was another glass on which the artist, Gordon Morison, had secretly worked in the names of a couple of his girlfriends. Gordon recalls doing the artwork: 'When I did that *Spiderman* game, rather than mess around, I took a tracing of the *Spiderman* comic and blew the thing up in size. It had to be okayed by Marvel Comics, so I took it to New York and their artist looked at it. He didn't realise it was *his* drawing and he made me make all these darned changes like lengthening a finger and so on. He even said I should have copied one of his drawings. I nearly told him "I don't copy – I trace!"'

During the 1970s Bally pioneered the celebrity pinballs. Pete Townshend and The Who wrote the rock opera *Tommy,* and in 1975 the movie of the same name was released starring Roger Daltrey, Ann-Margret, Oliver Reed, and Elton John, with script and direction by Ken Russell, who made this masterpiece with his usual blend of mystical photography, tricks, and effects working overtime. Millions flocked to see the movie and the *Tommy* record album sold well over

RIGHT *THE HUGELY TALENTED DOLLY PARTON AS DEPICTED BY DAVE CHRISTENSEN FOR BALLY IN 1979.*

Superstar Dolly Parton lights up Bally's newest flipper with her unmistakable style.

Dolly Parton Saucer and Target Feature
The top saucer and drop targets lite P-A-R-T-O-N, while the left targets lite D-O-L-L-Y to complete the center playfield D-O-L-L-Y P-A-R-T-O-N for points, special and replay. Values increase with each sequence completion.

Superstar In-Line Drop Targets
4 skill-shot multi-valued Superstar In-Line drop targets with 2x, 3x and 5x bonus multiplier provide players with challenging skill shots, while they also lite the spinner for extra points. These superstar targets spot the top P-A-R-T-O-N letters for points and then open to a Superstar Target for extra ball, special and 20,000 points.

Popular Ball Exit Feature
Right Center ball exit roll-over scores 5,000 points and returns the ball to the plunger for extra play.

Certified Gold Dolly Parton Hit Song
"Here You Come Again," one of Dolly's biggest hits plays during the game for extra entertainment pleasure.

3 Coin Chute Door

3 or 5 Ball Option

Convertible to add-a-ball

Automatic Self Test Switch

Bally

PINBALL DIVISION

90 O'Leary Drive, Bensenville, Illinois 60106, U.S.A.
Telephone: (312) 860-6400

PRINTED IN U.

10 million copies. Tommy, played by Roger Daltrey, was the now legendary 'Deaf, dumb and blind kid who sure played a mean pinball.' (The most famous song from the album, *Pinball Wizard*, had in fact been a hit record for The Who six years previously, back in early 1969. After the film was released it became a Top Ten hit for Elton John, who sang it in the movie.)

Capitalising on the release of the film, Bally concurrently brought out a new pinball game *Wizard*. Coinciding with the film's promotion, pinball tournaments were organised in music stores all over Chicago, sponsored by local radio stations. The teams featured celebrities, disc jockeys, athletes, and television personalities, and the finalists competed against each other at the Chicago Press Premier of *Tommy* at the State Lake Theatre. Promotional badges, Wizard and Tommy tee-shirts, record albums, and free tickets for the movie were all given away.

Wizard was an enormous success and at the time was Bally's best-ever seller. The impact of the artwork by Dave Christensen was immediate: the whole cabinet, playfield, and backglass were finished in predominantly bright yellow, red, and blue primary colours. The cabinet's ornate swirling artwork instantly attracted attention. The game itself, designed by Greg Kmiec, was a great favourite with players and remains highly collectable. On the painted backglass, centre screen, were the stars, Tommy in dark glasses and an Ann-Margret lookalike wearing a skimpy dress. Two sirens emerge from kickout saucers, and at the bottom of the glass is a large silver ball with 'Tommy' written on it, shackled to the leg of Ann-Margret. In other words, it was a winner.

The following year, riding high on the success of Wizard, Bally brought out another game based on a character from *Tommy*, this time featuring Elton John. *Captain Fantastic* was the name of the game, and the winning combination of Greg Kmiec's playfield design and Dave Christensen's brilliant artwork once again hit the jackpot for Bally. *Wizard* sold over 10,000 games, but *Captain Fantastic* sold more than half as many again, hitting a new sales record. The backglass depicted Elton John in his famous outsize Doc Marten's boots (which, incidentally, sold in 1988 at a Sotheby's rock n'roll memorabilia auction for over £12,000), and Christensen cleverly distorted the perspective as had been done in the movie during the *Pinball Wizard* sequence, to make Elton look about 10 feet tall.

This backglass really looks magnificent, and with the rest of the Christensen artwork on the playfield makes this machine one of the all-time greats. Parts of the backglass were silvered on the reverse, giving a mirror sparkle wherever it showed, an idea that had been repeated occasionally on many glasses for half a century (Bally's *Beauty* used it as long ago as 1940, and Williams more recently on *Black Knight* and *Firepower*). Also, the bumper caps had a picture of Elton John engraved into the plastic. (For many years bumper caps were a standard design used from game to game, but custom-designed caps became a feature of many later machines.)

Evil Knievel was a name which began to be heard on the news in the 1970s. He was one of those adventurers who have broken every bone in their bodies attempting to jump motorcycles over buses, or drive a car over the Grand Canyon. Whatever the logic, or lack of it, fame is assured by those who attempt to cheat death with self-inflicted feats of heroism – particularly if they fail. Anyway, Bally obviously thought Knievel would be around long enough to star in a 1977 pinball game.

Dolly Parton appeared two years later. The backglass artwork showed her at her curvaceous best singing into the microphone. The playfield had an unusual artwork arrangement because Dolly was depicted seated on one side of the playfield, and a large record was featured in the centre of the board, 'Superstar Dolly Parton lights up Bally's newest flipper with her unmistakable style', proclaimed the advertising flyer. Meanwhile, 'Here you come again', one of Dolly's biggest hits, played during the game.

Bally and RCA Records participated in a joint merchandising deal, Bally providing the new *Dolly Parton* pintable and RCA supplying the records and promotional material to record stores and radio stations to publicise her latest record, *Great Balls of Fire*. Radio listeners answering questions in a simple quiz won free records and the big prize, not Dolly herself, but the *Dolly Parton* pintable went to the winner of a grand draw. Dave Christensen was once again the artist on the game, though he had a few problems. He explained that, 'The Dolly Parton picture was done about three times. Her manager wanted to project her from a country and western artist into a sort of crossover artist so he kept changing it and changing it – we put one dress on her after another! It was quite a pretty game to look at, as were most of my later games like *Nitro Groundshaker*, but they were poor to play – more like 1960's games – basically because I wasn't given the

RIGHT *THOSE THREE FEMALE TELEVISION DETECTIVES, CHARLIE'S ANGELS, MADE IT BIG IN PINBALL IN 1978. (GORDON MORISON)*

Gottlieb's FOUR-PLAYER

CHARLIE'S ANGELS

ELTON JOHN WAS FEATURED ON BALLY'S BEST-SELLING
CAPTAIN FANTASTIC. BEHIND ELTON'S RIGHT FOOT A
COUPLE ARE ENGAGED IN A LITTLE LEWD HORSEPLAY.

best game designers in my last years with Bally.'

Playboy magnate Hugh Hefner had the unique distinction of having two pinballs bearing his image. The original 1978 Bally *Playboy* used artwork painted by Paul Faris, but the 1989 Data East game *Playboy* used a photographic backglass which, with the cost of the models, photographers, makeup people, etc. turned out to be a very expensive job. Photographic backglasses with real people are generally six to seven times more expensive than artwork. Incidentally, Hefner was pictured along with the 1988 Playmate of the Year, Kimberley Conrad, who shortly afterwards became his wife.

Artist Kevin O'Connor and chief designer Joe Kaminkow flew out to Hefner's Beverley Hills mansion for a meeting. As O'Connor recalls:

It was quite an experience. The grounds are spectacular with exotic animals and birds everywhere, and swimming pools and grottoes shaped out of the rock. We went up to the mansion and through the large hallway into the dining room and laid out our rough layouts on the table. I wondered whether Hefner would really appear in the legendary purple dressing gown and slippers but sure enough he did, and we had a real nice meeting. The photo-shoot was done in several stages. The first day we shot all the background, the waterfall, and Playboy models; the second day Hugh Hefner and Kimberley Conrad were photographed on their own; and then later they were amalgamated together with the cartoon rabbit and logo. The finished backglass came very close to my original conception on the rough sketch.

*LEFT VARIOUS CELEBRITIES TRIED TO HAIL A CAB ON WILLIAMS' FUN GAME, **TAXI**. (PYTHON ANGHELO)*

*RIGHT RONNIE AND NANCY REAGAN MADE A GUEST APPEARANCE ON THE WHITE-KNUCKLE RIDE, WILLIAMS' **CYCLONE** IN 1988. (PYTHON ANGHELO)*

The grand finale to the week's work was a fantasy party — a pyjama get-together at the Playboy mansion to which the Data East team, Kevin O'Connor, Joe Kaminkow, and Gary Stern were invited with movie stars, showbiz, and television personalities.

Celebrities do sometimes make a token appearance on pinball artwork. On Williams' *Cyclone*, Ronnie and Nancy Reagan are tightly gripping onto a white-knuckle roller coaster ride (courtesy of Williams' artist Python Anghelo), Nancy carries the message, 'Say No to drugs.' On a lighter note Williams' *Taxi* had President Gorbachev, Marilyn Monroe, Dracula, and Santa Claus as passengers queueing to catch a taxi cab!

One well-known person who was not welcomed by the Bally management was Adolf Hitler, who made a guest appearance in the crowd on Bally's *Captain Fantastic*. Artist Dave Christensen explained: 'I just put Hitler in the audience as a goofy idea. However, people at Bally said "What the hell is Adolf Hitler doing in the audience at an Elton John concert?" They couldn't figure out it was just a joke. I was labelled a fascist because of it!' Less controversial was James Bond, who appeared in a game which Gottlieb described as 'the pinball licensed to thrill' in 1980. Ideally suited to the adventurous spirit of pinball, the tongue-in-cheek action was once described as 'a comic strip for grown-ups'. The artwork by Doug Watson showed Roger Moore as Bond, inevitably surrounded by the Bond girls. This machine was unusual in that there was no limit to the number of balls available, but it was a timed game. The player had 50 time units at the start, and he competed against the clock with extra time units available through skilful play.

In 1989 Bally came up with a great new fun game. *Elvira and the Party Monsters* was the latest in celebrity tie-ins, packed with novel features such as the boogie men (little rubber monsters who danced on the playfield) and the skull cave (shooting 3 balls energises the Crypt Kicker — the phantom organist breaks into a wild solo, the brilliant light show begins and the spirits yell 'party!'). The game also featured the novel jumper bumpers, which had caps that went up and down with the bumper action.

Elvira found fame as a spoof-horror queen who gained a cult following. The heroine dresses entirely in black, including black back-combed hair, with heavy black eye-liner and black fingernails, but her most sensational gimmick is the very low-cut, atomic dress with plenty of fall-out! So much so, in fact, that the manufacturers provide a special kit for conservative locations enabling you to cover up the cleavage. There

is an additional special sound option 'to protect the eyes and ears of the little party monsters'. Elvira's suggestive comments are also cut out.

Greg Freres, who did the artwork, explains: 'We had a lot of fun doing this one. Elvira was just great to work with; everything was positive and when you get a good cohesive group working in harmony it comes through on the game. We'd been thinking of doing a follow-up to *Party Animal*, then the management came up with this idea so we said, "Let's marry the two together as her persona is a kind of fun character."'

Elvira also involved some extra characters. On a plastic light shield is a Frankenstein character carrying a pile of pizza boxes, one of which has written on it 'Tony and Barb', a reference to pinball artist Tony Ramunni and his wife. Greg explained: 'When Elvira saw the artwork for the playfield, she saw me saying "Hi" to all these people in the artwork, so she wanted me to do the same thing on the backglass. She sent me a bunch of requests to say "Hi" to different people. You can see her holding a hot-dog on a barbecue fork that says "I ♡ Smarkie", — a reference to her husband/manager Mark. There's also a ghoulish reference on a tombstone to Yogi Travis, a guy she used to play pinball with way back.' The game designer Denis Nordman posed for the werewolf character on the backglass, while designer Jim Patla posed for Dracula, and artist Tim Elliott is the muscleman.

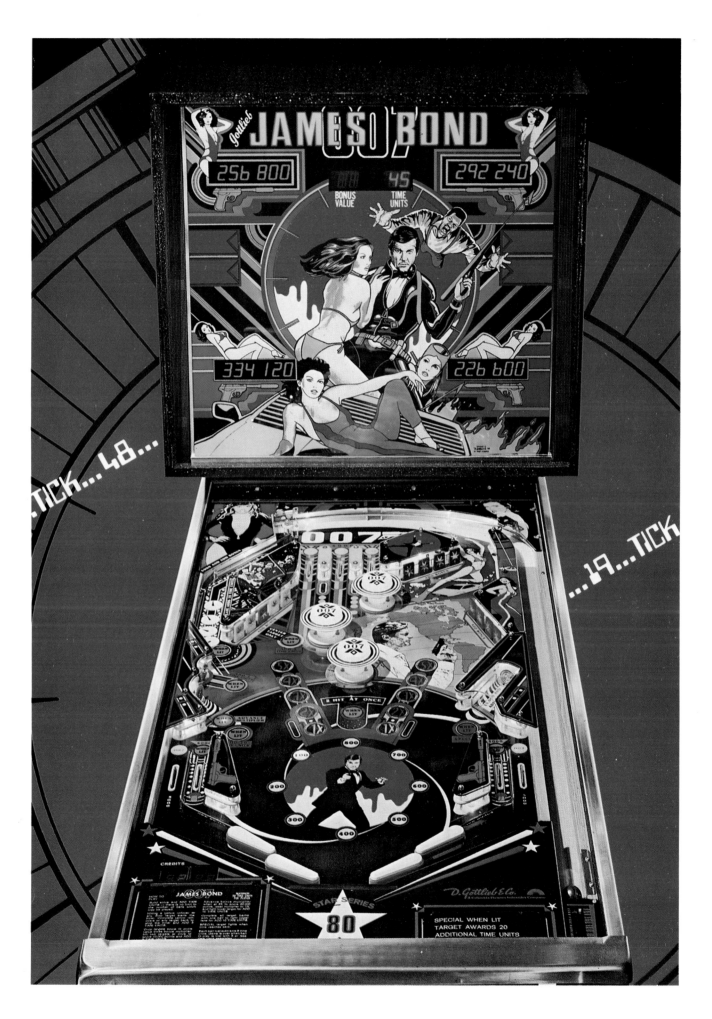

When They Named A Game After Me, It Had To Be Built!

ELVIRA

I told the boys that Bally's "Elvira" had to be good . . . and it is! Players can't keep their hands off my new game! Everywhere you look, big beautiful features beg for attention—Pinball has never been so good or so satisfying! Believe me, everybody scores big with Elvira and the Party Monsters. The profits and the action begin with my name . . .

Spelling E·L·V·I·R·A lights the skull cave for 3 million points and ignites player excitement! This timed feature forces players to perform under pressure—and that's just the way I like it!

The ALL NEW Skull Cave.
High-Spirited Multiball Action Starts Here!

Shooting 3 balls into the Skull Cave energizes the Crypt kicker, and suddenly, the entire playfield is veiled in a shroud of darkness. When the phantom organist breaks into a wild solo, the brilliant light show begins, spirits yell, "PARTY!" and one . . . two . . . three balls soar out of the crypt, fly through the air and come in for a crash landing in the "Jumper Bumper" zone. Players who really know how to party can collect the Party Monster Jackpot! It starts at 1,000,000 points and keeps building during multi-ball madness. Players must have at least two balls in play and make both ramps to collect their prize.

ALL NEW *Jumper Bumpers*. A Bally Pinball Exclusive! Players Get More Action Than Ever Before!

Guess what! These caps jump up and down with high-powered solonoid action. I'm the first to give players the vertical action they've been waiting for! While building the "Boogie Bonus," Jumper Bumpers add to the score and keep players coming back for more!

Flip-Up Targets.
All New Visual Excitement!

Players get a rise out of me and my buddy, Drac, with shots strong enough to lift the lids on our coffins. When the Count awakens, he's always in the mood for a bite to eat. And it's in the player's best interest to light the barbecue and collect a big bonus . . . before the Count sinks his teeth into something other than hamburger meat!

*SPOOF HORROR FUN AND GAMES FROM BALLY WITH **ELVIRA AND THE PARTY MONSTERS**. (GREG FRERES)*

Sounds That Go Bump In The Night!

Let me whisper in your ear! Yes, it's really my voice that's calling out to your players! The Count and I shout encouraging words while an all-original musical score brings out the demon in every player!

Elvira Is No Cheap Date!

Players will pay to play with me! It takes more than a quarter to turn me on! One chance to party with Yours Cruelly costs 50¢ ...and nobody argues! Players who come back for more get a deal...two rounds with me costs 75¢, and players who really have stamina can play three for a $1.00!

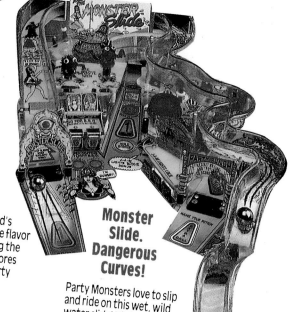

LL NEW Boogie Men. ve Entertainment!

ese awesome party monsters have players eaming with delight! When the music and light w begin, the Boogie men really get down. ers will do almost anything to see these little devils dance! Besides one heck of a show, e's a rewarding Boogie Bonus too!

Party Punch!

The secret ingredient is me—it's the world's tastiest punch—and players can add to the flavor by stirring in their own ingredients. Making the right ramp opens the potion pantry and scores big points with Elvira! I reward the best Party Monsters with an extra ball!

Deadheads

Put on your rockin' shoes. It's no easy task to wake the dead—Players must visit the graveyard and complete all four tombstone targets just to get one of these spirits to stir. Arousing all 3 Deadheads lights the eject hole for 1 million points!

Monster Slide. Dangerous Curves!

Party Monsters love to slip and ride on this wet, wild water slide! High-speed action sends balls careening through dangerous twists and curves on their way to the exclusive Downhill-Uphill ramp. With a motion that defies gravity, balls travel downhill and then back up! Consecutive slide shots keep building values to 1 million!

Incorporating references to people in the artwork is by no means a new idea, and one of the earliest instances occurred in 1949 on Williams' *Freshie*. The glass showed young couples flirting on a college campus. On a fence were three lovers' hearts, each with two sets of initials. These were the initials of company founder Harry Williams and his daughter Kitchie, Sam Stern and his wife Ellie, and Williams' chief designer Gordon Horlock and his wife.

One of the most neglected areas of early pinball art was pop music. In 1956, during an American radio programme, Asa Carter of the White Citizens Council broadcast these words: 'Rock and roll is a plot to undermine the morals of the youth of our nation, and is sexualistic and unmoralistic (sic).' Similar statements were often levelled at pinball machines and they were

sentiments guaranteed to make teenagers even more committed to pinball. The person who started the furore was Bill Haley (with *The Comets*) singing 'Shake, rattle and roll'. Rock 'n'roll did, however, eventually gain respectability and even better a place in the history books. Yet strangely, no 1950's pinball machine ever featured a rock 'n'roller. The nearest it got was with *Hot Diggity* by Williams in 1956.

'THE BOOTLES' WAS THE NAME GIVEN TO THIS POP GROUP BY ARTIST JERRY K. KELLEY AT THE HEIGHT OF BEATLEMANIA IN 1967.

However, come 1963 this did not matter. Rock 'n'roll was obsolete overnight. All the Bobbies (Darin, Vee, Vinton, etc.) and the likes of Fabian and Rick Nelson were about to be replaced by a precocious new model. Beatlemania hit the world in 1963, and suddenly there was a demand for all things Beatle. Williams eventually responded with *Beat Time*, although this did not appear until 1967. This was one of the games Jerry Kelley painted for Williams, and it is drawn in his unique, modern style. The backglass featured a stylised mop-headed pop group singing 'Ya Ya Ya Ya Ya Ya', and its name on the drummer's bass – the *BOOTLES*. Still, everyone knew who it was supposed to be, and there were no problems with licensing or authorisation.

This ploy had parallels in the record industry. On the back of Beatlemania rode numerous cheap rip-off records which could easily be mistaken for the real thing, where misspelling of the name *Beatle* should have been obvious to even the youngest record buyers. The Beetle Beat was the title of one, and Beattle Mash another, all featuring lookalikes of John, Paul, George, and Ringo on the cover. About this time five young musicians from south London formed themselves into what was to become the greatest rock band in the history of pop music, The Rolling Stones. Messrs Jagger, Jones, Watts, Wyman, and Richards started their musical careers rebelling against the standard pop of the day. Their musical roots stretched back to black American R & B, and they started to make a name for themselves peddling British versions of the likes of Chuck Berry and Bo Diddley.

*THE **ROLLING STONES** GATHERED SOME MOSS FOR BALLY IN 1980. (GREG FRERES)*

The Stones presented a decadent long-haired image to the world. Working on the premise that the quickest way to a teenager's heart is by offending his parents, the group's managers (Eric Easton and Andrew Loog Oldham) steered their careers through sex and drug scandals to the very pinnacle of teenage idolatry. The *Los Angeles Times* wrote about them: 'They're perverted, outrageous, ugly, tasteless and incoherent – that's what's so good about them.' Fame was assured. In 1980 they took their places in the Pinball Hall of Fame, when Bally brought out *Rolling Stones*. Greg Freres worked on the graphics and explains, 'The licence originated with the marketing director at Bally, Tom Nieman, who'd been successful with *Kiss* and *The Harlem Globetrotters*. Tom was going licence crazy at that time so we said, "Why not put the greatest rock n'roll band in the world on a backglass?" The Stones didn't play much part in the production, and the artwork was done from whatever photographs and books I could get hold of – not very good reference!'

Another source of inspiration was the heavy metal group Kiss, whose gimmick was painted faces, a cross between aboriginal art and 1930s deco. They also had an aggressive licensing and merchandising company, Boutwell-Aucoin. Always hungry for promotion, in 1978 they contacted Bally's Tom Nieman, and invited him to see the boys in action at a concert in the Chicago Stadium, with a view to creating a game based on their act. Tom said, 'I was impressed and got our chief artist Paul Faris to go along and see them. He checked the group out and *Kiss* was on the way.'

All the artwork had to be approved by the band. Pedantic with their makeup and costumes, they had to approve all the details down to the length of their hair and even the size of their over-emphasised, rippling body muscles. The one problem that did arise concerned the stencils for the cabinet. Normally one stencil is used on the side of the cabinet and then turned over for a reversed image on the opposite side. However, guitarist Paul Stanley's makeup has a big star around his right eye so he was in danger of having it over the left eye using this technique. Bally, therefore, had to make a whole new set of stencils for the opposite side of the cabinets. Kevin O'Connor, the artist who worked on *Kiss*, is reputed to have got the artwork for the backglass right at the first attempt. The glass captured the real essence of the band and featured a strobelight

effect which flashed the letters 'K-I-S-S' in sequence, emulating the Kiss logo used in the stage act. (Two evangelical ministers, incidentally, had once declared that Kiss was an acronym for 'Kids in the service of Satan', decrying rock n'roll as the devil's music!)

Back in 1976 Kiss dressed up in weird black leather and used makeup, an essential part of the act. They had said at the time, 'If we took the makeup off it would be a different band. That doesn't mean the band would end. Like the caterpillar turning into the butterfly we would simply change form and go endlessly on through the Milky Way.' By 1990, like the butterfly, they had changed form and abandoned their makeup and grown their hair even longer for their first hit in 14 years, 'Forever'. Will we see a new pinball machine with a re-designed backglass – minus makeup – *Kiss II*? In the meantime, *Kiss* is one of Bally's better games and looks like achieving classic pinball status and desirability as the ultimate Kiss collectible. In the 21st century it will no doubt sell in international auction room memorabilia sales for handsome sums of money.

Another recent Bally solid rock hit is *Heavy Metal Meltdown*. The designers really went for the big one. The artwork by Tony Ramunni featured a group of long-haired, heavy metal idols sporting flamboyantly decorated electric guitars. One cynic described the game plan as so simple 'that even your average headbanger could get to grips with it before he'd spent the price of a Def Leppard album.' The game's title had a double meaning, also referring to having up to five balls simultaneously in play. The description ran 'You're in control of some hot licks – you're the star.' The backbox was surmounted by 'awesome stacks', actually a couple of small loudspeakers from which emerged 'screaming guitar solos with every ball in play!' Pinball had certainly come a long way since *Baffle Ball* 60 years ago. The early designers could never have dreamt someone would say of a pinball, 'If it's too loud you're too old.'

In the world of sporting personalities the list of great American boxing champions is endless – there are the legendary names of Joe Louis, Rocky Marciano, Floyd Patterson, George Foreman, Joe Frazier and Mike Tyson, but probably the most memorable is the self-acclaimed greatest, Muhammed Ali. In one of his finest

*STERN'S PROMOTIONAL BROCHURE FOR **ALI** DEPICTED THE GREAT MAN RECITING HIS POETRY. (BOB TIMS)*

*THE **ROCKY** PINBALL WAS FEATURED IN 'ROCKY III', ONE OF THE SERIES OF FILMS THAT TOOK SYLVESTER STALLONE TO SUPERSTARDOM. (DAVID A. MOORE)*

fights he met Frazier at Madison Square Garden on March 8th, 1971, sharing $5 million for the first televised superfight, watched by an estimated audience of 300 million people in 46 countries. It is a pity for Stern Electronics that they did not all rush out and buy Stern's 1979 pinball *Ali*. It might have helped prevent Stern closing the doors on its pinball division five years later! The pinball *Ali* had what you could call a knockout backglass, with the face of 'The Greatest' pictured in the centre surrounded by several smaller cameo pictures of himself.

The *Rocky* series of films, starring the not-as-tough Sylvester Stallone, propelled the actor into the megastar bracket. The original *Rocky* had been a low budget film and Stallone was an unknown until it won an Academy Award. Gottlieb's 1982 *Rocky* featured the sound of the bell and the roar of the crowd, and had bonus lanes such as 'upper cut' and 'knockout punch'. As the bell rang the end of each round the machine taunts players with 'You lost – ha ha!'

The artwork on the *Rocky* backglass depicted Stallone with his arms held aloft in a victory stance, while in the background the floodlit boxing ring and capacity crowd are jumping out of their seats with excitement. The flipper arrangement on this machine was unusual, with one conventionally arranged pair on the left at the bottom (labelled left jab and right hook) and another conventional pair at the bottom right (labelled left hook and right jab).

The Pinball Hall of Fame could justifiably include many of those who have been fired into space. In fact they are better represented in pinball by the machines and missions on which they travelled. The history of space travel began when in 1961 the Russians scored a major first when Major Yuri Gagarin blasted into the history books with a one-orbit journey into space and around the earth. The handsome Gagarin became a world celebrity and the London tabloid newspapers carried headlines such as 'Girls go Ga-Ga over Gagarin'. Meanwhile America had still not put a man into orbital flight. The Freedom 7 and Liberty Belle 7 were both up and down flights, what Soviet Premier Nikita Kruschev scornfully referrred to as a 'flea jump'. The first American orbital flight came on February 20th, 1962. John Glenn in a Mercury/Atlas vehicle went into an elliptical orbit of 100 by 160 miles. His capsule was called 'Friendship 7'. Over Australia Glenn reported seeing lights – the city of Perth had turned them full on in his honour. After three orbits Glenn returned to a hero's welcome from a proud America.

Both Williams and Gottlieb seized the opportunity to pay their own tribute. Gottlieb brought out their four-player *Liberty Belle*, in February 1962, and Williams brought out *Friendship 7*, an add-a-ball game in July 1962. *Friendship 7* had the usual brightly coloured artwork that was typical of Williams in the early 1960s, and in spite of being a serious subject still incorporated some of the comic art of the period. The backglass featured the Friendship 7 capsule re-entering the earth's atmosphere, surrounded by swirls of multi-coloured vapour, and in the lower left-hand corner astronaut

RIGHT THIS BROCHURE FOR WILLIAMS' 1959 GAME **ROCKET** HERALDED THE DAWNING OF THE SPACE-AGE.

BELOW ARTIST GORDON MORISON PRESENTED A HUMOROUS VIEW OF SPACE TRAVEL ON GOTTLIEB'S 1979 GAME, **COUNTDOWN**.

Williams
ROCKET

(1)
SELECT
(2)
COUNT-DOWN
(3)
FIRE!

"ORBIT" any 3 successive Rockets for "Special"!

3 to 7-IN-LINE SCORING!

TESTED FOR 16 WEEKS
APPROVED AND RECOMMENDED
ON 25 LOCATIONS

ROCKET   ROCKET

John Glenn smiles inside his spacesuit. On the playfield the capsule is shown at the very top, and just above the flippers the people in the street are looking skywards in wonder. The plastic lightshields show the Atlas rocket and scenes inside the tracking station. It was altogether an attractive package, and much more realistic than Williams' 1961 *Spaceship*. This artwork was somewhat frivolous compared with the real thing, and there were several young girls floating around in space wearing mini-skirted spacesuits and goldfish bowl helmets!

Astronaut Virgil Grisson had once said, 'If we die, we want people to accept it, we're in a risky business. The conquest of space is worth the risk of life.' In January 1967 he did indeed lose his life along with fellow astronauts Edward White and Roger Chaffee when a flash fire swept through their flight capsule in a simulated countdown for the Apollo 1 flight. Williams launched the pinball *Apollo* in that same year, just a few months after the fatal fire and just weeks before Von Braun's moon rocket, the Saturn V (Apollo 4) was rolled out onto the launch pad to send an unmanned space capsule into orbit.

Williams' *Apollo* was a very popular game with its open playfield design. Williams also brought out an add-a-ball version called *Blast Off* with similar artwork. The backglass showed the rocket on its launch pad with the control tower nearby. The centre of the playfield was occupied from top to bottom by a large Saturn V rocket painted on the board, with 10 rollover buttons along its length. Incorporated in the backbox was a miniature vertical pintable (like the early bagatelles with real metal pins). A ball leaving the playfield would launch a small ball in the miniature playfield to score an extra 50 points, 300 points, or a 'Special', the ball being launched from the nose of the spacecraft on the glass.

Two other games using the space theme include: Williams' *Strato-Flite* (1974) which depicted a delta-winged supersonic airliner, vaguely reminiscent of Concorde, streaking through the stratosphere. And Williams' *Space Mission* (1976) carried a picture of the combined American and Russian spacecraft, Apollo and Soyuz docked together, in a symbiotic relationship as they had been in July the previous year.

By the time of the bicentennial celebrations in 1976, the space theme was again all important. Gottlieb's contribution was *Spirit of '76* which illustrated the old and new in juxtaposition. Davy Crockett is shown complete with famous hat standing behind an astronaut in full space gear. Gottlieb's *Pioneer* of the same year showed the Saturn rocket blasting a path to the stars symbolising America's greatest achievements.

On April 12th, 1981, yet another historic vehicle took off into space from the reclaimed swampland of the Kennedy Space Centre. This was the maiden flight of the first space shuttle Columbia. Columbia's launch on that sunny April morning was not only a triumphant demonstration of the commitment to space exploration, but a celebration. It was 20 years to the day since the Soviet cosmonaut Yuri Gagarin had become the first man in space. There was only one cause for concern. The crew subsequently had reported losing some of the ceramic tiles covering the upper tail section – they did not know if any were missing underneath, and there was an anxious 21 minutes of radio blackout during re-entry. Columbia hit the atmosphere travelling at 25 times the speed of sound, far faster than any other winged aircraft had done before. But all was well. The re-usable spacecraft became a reality.

It was not until 1984 that the first space shuttle was launched on a pinball glass. Williams brought out its Space Shuttle which was novel because it incorporated a small plastic model of the shuttle on the playfield. It was a winner for Williams which was looking for a sales boost. The Italian manufacturer, Zaccaria, also brought out a great looking version of *Space Shuttle*. The colouring of the Zaccaria artwork was reminiscent of Bally's *Fireball* with the cabinet and backglass finished predominantly in electric blue, setting off the bright reds, yellows, and oranges of the lettering and powered bumpers. Strangely, on the glass itself, the shuttle vehicle is mounted on the back of a jet-liner instead of a rocket. This was actually the prototype orbiter Enterprise (named after the illustrious spaceship in *Star Trek*) which during testing in 1977 used to fly piggy-back style on top of a Boeing 747 over the Mojave Desert in California, before separating and gliding to a runway landing at the Edwards Air Force base.

Needless to say none of man's space journeys have approached the interstellar adventures of Captain Kirk and his crew in the starship Enterprise, (powered by a matter/anti-matter reaction at warp speeds, faster than light itself). Bally brought out a pinball machine *Star Trek* in 1979 hoping to appeal to a huge following of 'Trekkies' who were addicted to watching the 78 episodes that were made. The artwork on the backglass, superbly painted by Kevin O'Connor, showed Kirk and Spock and the crew on a faraway planet with the Enterprise hovering in the background.

*WILLIAMS' **SPACE SHUTTLE** FEATURED A MODEL OF THE SHUTTLE ON THE PLAYFIELD. (MARK SPRENGER)*

CHAPTER 6

REVELATION

From the earliest days of pinball the screen-printing process was used for the artwork decoration. Initially, the simple patterns were screen-printed onto thin films which could be soaked in water, slid off the backing, and affixed to the machine (the decals were similar to the water transfers that children sometimes use.)

Ray Moloney, founder of the Bally Corporation, was the person credited with asking Tom Grant (who ran Advertising Posters) to investigate the possibility of printing onto glass. Grant found it was possible and the painted backglass was in business. It was then just a short step to lighting it from behind to give that familiar, warm, soft glow.

The screen process is a method of printing which applies colours through a series of cut-out stencils, the stencils being affixed to a fine, stretched mesh made of polyester. In the case of pinball playfields and back-glasses a series of up to 16 colours (called inks in the trade) are applied in succession, each coat being allowed to dry, so building up the complete picture. The mesh holding the stencil is held in contact with the playfield or glass, and the ink is spread over the mesh and stencil using a plastic bladed squeegee which drives it through the mesh depositing it in a thin, even layer.

Accurate registration is called for, although inevitably there are overlaps and in the case of the glass, overlaps can form an extra colour. For instance, a blue and yellow overlapping can form a green different to the main green chosen for the piece.

Today the process is largely automated. When all the colours have been laid down on a playfield, an artist retouches any small blemishes using fine sable brushes before the playfield is given its final transparent hard-coat, the lacquer that protects the inks from the hammering of the steel ball during tens of thousands of games. This hardcoat is crucial. Advertising Posters spent considerable time and money perfecting this and it gave them a monopoly for years. Other companies tried to copy it but the paintwork would break down very quickly if the same material was not used. Paul Faris was involved at Bally in developing an alternative hardcoat using ultra-violet curing materials, but it was not successful.

The playfield goes through the following seven stages:

BELOW SCREENS BEING PREPARED IN A MODERN SCREEN-PRINTING PLANT. (COURTESY OF SUN PROCESS)

BELOW LEFT *THE SEALED AND SANDED PLAYFIELD OF WILLIAMS'* **RIVERBOAT GAMBLER** *ABOUT TO RECEIVE ITS FIRST PASS OF INK. EACH COAT AIR-DRIES IN ABOUT 1 HOUR. (COURTESY OF SUN PROCESS)*

BELOW RIGHT *THE FINISHED PLAYFIELDS ARE RACKED READY FOR PACKING AND SHIPPING. ON DISPLAY IS A SAMPLE BOARD. (COURTESY OF SUN PROCESS)*

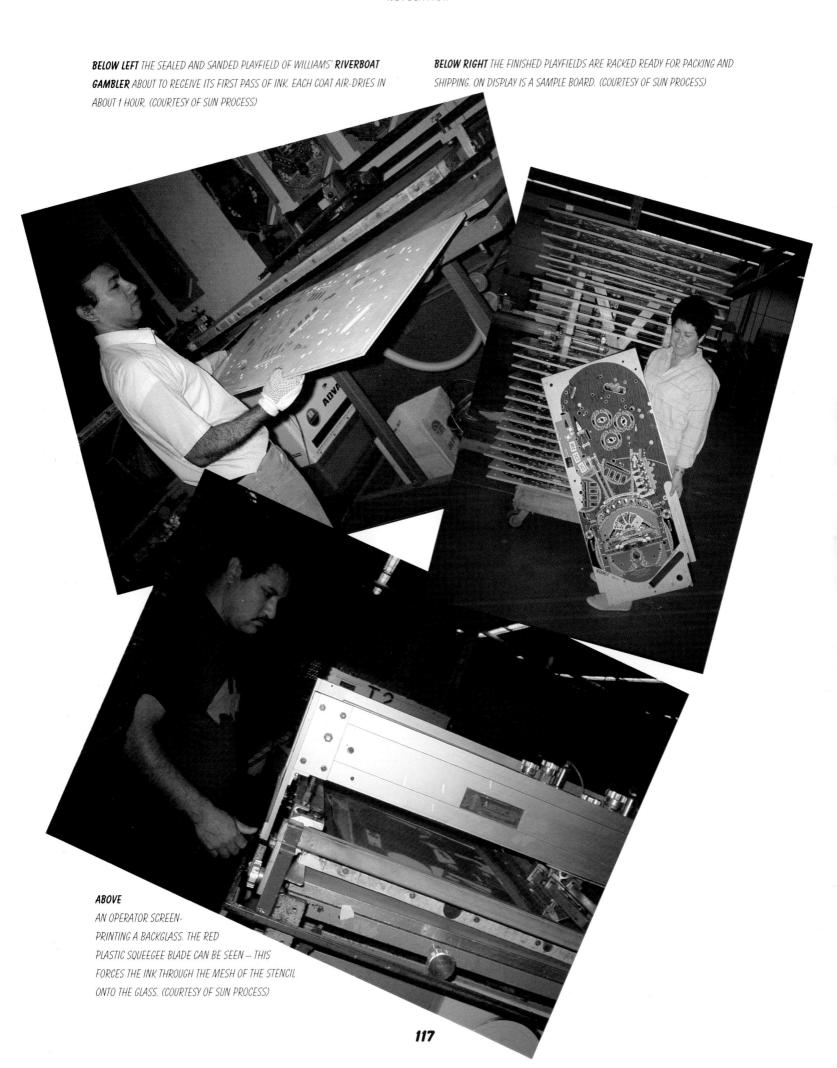

ABOVE

AN OPERATOR SCREEN-PRINTING A BACKGLASS. THE RED PLASTIC SQUEEGEE BLADE CAN BE SEEN – THIS FORCES THE INK THROUGH THE MESH OF THE STENCIL ONTO THE GLASS. (COURTESY OF SUN PROCESS)

● The wooden playfields arrive from the supplier already drilled and routed, and fitted wth plastic light covers. They are inspected by the quality control department.

● The boards are put through the sanding room where all the edges and rough surfaces are smoothed with automatic sanders.

● Both sides of the playfield boards are sprayed with a matt transparent primer/sealer to prevent water absorption, and to prevent the subsequent layers of ink soaking in.

● The boards are returned to the sanding room where they are gently hand-sanded to remove small raised areas from the sealing process.

● The printing begins with a first layer of white ink over the entire graphic area which is allowed to dry (this gives the subsequent coloured layers greater luminosity and vibrancy).

● From 8–16 coloured layers are applied one at a time. Each coat takes one hour to dry.

● After any imperfections have been retouched, the playfield goes through the computerised spray booth to receive its final transparent lacquer hardcoat to protect the printed surface.

The backglasses are printed in exactly the same way, except the colours are applied to the reverse of the glass and in reverse order, the black outlines being applied first. A flood coat of white is applied to the back of the colours to diffuse the light from the bulbs and bring out the vibrancy of the colours. A final opaque silver coat is then screen-printed over those areas of the glass which will not be illuminated. The playfield uses conventional printing inks, but the glasses use photosensitive inks which are run through an ultra-violet light after printing which dries it immediately. The first game made with these inks was Bally's *Lost World* in 1978.

Sometimes areas of the glass are given a mirrored finish. This adds considerably to the cost of the glass. The glass sheets arrive at the printing shop completely mirrored, and then a special etching process removes the areas not wanted on the glass.

It can be seen that the initial setting up of the

equipment for just one game involves a considerable amount of work, but once the screens are all made then the actual printing is a straightforward affair and can be completed fairly quickly.

Interestingly, Bally's *Lost World* was also the first game to use the newly developed four-colour process. A transparency of the artwork is put onto a laser scanner which breaks down the image into dots of four colours, which is then printed onto a glass or translucent plastic sheet. This is backlit in the pinball backbox in the conventional way. The advantage of this process is that subtle tonal gradations can be achieved which were only partially possible using the conventional screen-printing method.

Today the two systems comfortably co-exist, but the pinball purists will always prefer the brighter, brasher screen-printed glasses. It suits those comic characters that they have come to love so much, like *Humpty Dumpty*, *Square Head*, *Teacher's Pet*, *Jungle Queen*, *Fireball*, and *Gorgar*. They represent nostalgia, a time that is now history and gone forever – when the world was young and so were we. They are really what pinball art is all about.

THE ASSEMBLED PLAYFIELD LOOKS VERY DIFFERENT WITH ITS TARGETS, LIGHTSHIELDS AND BUMPERS ALL IN PLACE – THE END PRODUCT OF A LONG PROCESS!

APPENDIX 1
THE MEN AND THEIR MACHINES

The following is a chronological list of the principal artists who have worked on pinball art since World War II, together with the better known games for which they provided the artwork.

ROY PARKER

As far as is known he painted virtually every Gottlieb pinball machine from before World War II until approximately 1966. Here are just a few classics from his vast output:
Humpty Dumpty (1947), Knockout (1950), Coronation (1952), Dragonnette (1954), Criss Cross (1958), Lightning Ball (1959), Flipper (1960), Egghead (1961), Slick Chick (1963), Square Head (1963), Gigi (1963), World Fair (1964), Majorettes (1964), Skyline (1965), Ice Revue (1965), Mayfair (1966 – Parker's last game). He also worked on these Chicago Coin games: Kilroy (1947), Playboy (1947), Goldball (1947), Catalina (1948), Trinadad (1948), Firecracker (1963), and probably others.
Also many Genco games.

GEORGE MOLENTIN

Started working for Advertising Posters in 1935. From 1946 until 1961 he freelanced on practically all of the Williams' graphics. In 1961 he became art director of Advertising Posters, supervising approximately five artists, until retiring in 1979.
Freshie (1949), Spark Plugs (1951), Big Ben (1954), Jigsaw (1957), Turf Champ (1958), Gusher (1958), Casino (1958), 4 Stars (1958), Satellite (1958), Crossword (1959), Rocket (1959), Darts (1960), Golden Gloves (1960), Bobo (1961), Magic City (1967).
Worked on many Bally, United, Exhibit Supply and some Chicago Coin games during the 1940s and 1950s.

OSCAR SOLNER

Created some artwork for the Exhibit Supply Company.

ART STENHOLM

Worked for Advertising Posters from 1964 to 1971.

Gottlieb: North Star (1964), Cross Town (1966), Super Score (1967), Harmony (1967), Royal Guard (1968), Paul Bunyan (1968), Domino (1968), Spin-A-Card (1969), Mibs (1969), Road Race (1969), Aquarius (1970).
Bally: Bus Stop (1964), Mad World (1964).
Williams: Heatwave (1964), Stop N'Go (1964), Eager Beaver (1965), Moulin Rouge (1965).

JERRY K. KELLEY

Williams: Pot O' Gold (1965), A-Go-Go (1966), Beat Time (1967).
Bally: Capersville (1966), The Wiggler (1967), Dogies (1968), Rock Makers (1968), On Beam (1969), Cosmos (1969), Mariner (1971).

CHRISTIAN MARCHE

Worked for Advertising Posters from 1964 to 1978.
Williams: Apollo (1967), Daffie (1968), Doozie (1968), Smart Set (1969), Paddock (1969), Cue-T (1969), Miss 'O' (1969), Strike Zone (1970), Jive Time (1970), Zodiac (1971), Jackpot (1971), Klondike (1971), Doodle Bug (1971), Super Star (1972), Travel Time (1973), Triple Action (1974), Strato-Flite (1974), Oxo (1974), Toledo (1975), Space Mission (1976), World Cup (1978), Disco Fever (1978), Tri-Zone (1979).
Bally: Rocket III (1967), Dixieland (1968), Op-Pop-Pop (1969), Time Zone (1973), Bow and Arrow (1975), Hokus Pokus (1976).
Chicago Coin: Beatniks (1967), Twinky (1967), Moon Shot (1969), Hi Score Pool (1971), Casino (1972), Gold Record (1975), Juke Box (1976), and many more.

GORDON MORISON

Gottlieb: Roller Coaster (1971), Flying Carpet (1972), King Rock (1972), Space Orbit (1972), Jack-in-the-Box (1973), Royal Pair (1974),

Magnotron (1974), Spirit of '76 (1976), Card Whiz (1976), Surf Champ (1976), Cleopatra (1977), Jet Spin (1977), Jungle Queen (1977), Close Encounters (1978), Charlies Angels (1978), Eye of the Tiger (1978), Sinbad (1978), Buck Rogers (1979), Incredible Hulk (1979), Torch (1980), Spiderman (1980), Roller Disco (1980), and many more.

DICK WHITE

Bally: King Tut (1969), Vampire (1971), 4 Million BC (1971), Circus (1973), Nip-It (1973), Flicker (1975).
Wico: Big Top (1977).
Game Plan: Coney Island (1979).

DAVID CHRISTENSEN

Bally: Fireball (1972), Monte Carlo (1973), Odds N'Evens (1973), Ro Go (1974), Bon Voyage (1974), Wizard (1975), Air Aces (1975), Captain Fantastic (1976), Old Chicago (1976), Mata Hari (1978), Power Play (1978), Dolly Parton (1979), Groundshaker (1980), Fireball II (1981), Fireball Home Version (1981).

PAUL FARIS

Bally: Night Rider (1977), Eight Ball (1977), Playboy (1978), Lost World (1978), Paragon (1979), Xenon (1980), Space Invaders (1980), Centaur (1981).
Game Plan: Andromeda (1985).
Data East: Phantom of the Opera (1990).

GEORGE OPPERMAN

Atari: Time 2000 (1977), Airborne Avengers (1977), Superman (1978).

KEVIN O'CONNOR

Bally: Strikes and Spares (1978), Kiss (1979), Star Trek (1979), Silverball Mania (1980), Mystic (1980), Viking (1980), Flash Gordon (1981), Medusa (1981).
Data East: Lazer War (1987), Torpedo Alley (1988), Secret Service (1988), Playboy (1989).

TONY RAMUNNI

Williams: Black Knight (1980), Alien Poker (1980), Scorpion (1980).
Bally: Embryon (1981), Spy Hunter (1984), Eight Ball Classic (1985), Special Force (1986), Heavy Metal Meltdown (1987).

Mr Game: World Cup '90 (1990), Mac Attack (1990).

GREG FRERES

Bally: Harlem Globetrotters (1979), Frontier (1980), Skateball (1980), Rolling Stones (1980), Fathom (1981), BMX (1982), Vector (1982), Strange Science (1986), Hardbody (1987), Escape from the Lost World (1988), Elvira (1989).

CONSTANTINO MITCHELL

Williams: Flash (1979), Stellar Wars (1979), Time Warp (1979), Gorgar (1979), Laser Ball (1979), Firepower (1980), Blackout (1980), Thunderball (1983), Firepower II (1984).
Gottlieb: Lights, Camera, Action (1989), Excalibur (1989).

DOUG WATSON

Gottlieb: Panthera (1980), James Bond (1980), Devils Dare (1982).
Williams: Barracora (1981), F 14 Tomcat (1987), Black Knight 2000 (1989), Pool Sharks (1990).
Bally: Fireball Classic (1985), Bally Cybernaut (1985).

PAT McMAHON

Bally: Mr & Mrs Pacman (1982) X's and O's (1984), Atlantis (1989), Truck Stop (1989), Rollergames (1989).

JOHN YOUSSI

Williams: Whirlwind (1989), Police Force (1989) with Python Anghelo.
Bally: Radical (1990).

PYTHON ANGHELO

Williams: Comet (1985), High Speed (1986), Pinbot (1986), Big Guns (1987), Cyclone (1988), Taxi (1989), Jokerz (1989), Bad Cats (1989).

TERRY DOERZAPH

Gottlieb: Black Hole (1981), Haunted House (1982).

MARGARET HUDSON

Bally: Eight Ball de Luxe (1981), Pac-Man (1982), Granny and the Gators (1984), The Simpsons (1990).

SEAMUS McLAUGHLIN
Game Plan: Cyclops (1985), Loch Ness Monster (1985).

MARK SPRENGER
Williams: Space Shuttle (1984), Fire (1987), Banzai Run (1988), Diner (1989).

TIM ELLIOT
Williams: Road Kings (1986), Earthshaker (1989).
Bally: Transporter (1989), Game Show (1990).

DAVID A. MOORE
Gottlieb: Mars (1981), Rocky (1982), Punk (1982) with Terry Doerzaph, Vegas (1989) with Constantino Mitchell.

APPENDIX 2
PINBALL MILESTONES

A MISCELLANY OF PINBALL FACTS AND TRIVIA

1931
- The first coin-operated bagatelle games, Whiffle and Whoopee, are marketed.
- David Gottlieb introduced Baffle Ball, the first successful pinball game to sell over 50,000 machines.

1932
- Ray Moloney's Ballyhoo sold 75,000 machines.

1933
- For the first time batteries were used to provide illumination for scoring lights, initially on the playfield.
- Rockola's Juggle-Ball introduced the first player control. A moveable rod enabled the player to manipulate the course of the ball.
- Harry Williams invented the first electrically operated 'electric action' kickout hole. First used on Pacific Amusements' game Contact. Subsequently widely copied by other manufacturers. Contact also had a bell which rang when the kicker operated, making this the first sound action pinball.
- Bally's Airway was the first game to use automatic score bars at the bottom of a machine.
- Bally's Jack and Jill featured two side-by-side playfields, with separate ball lifts and plungers and one common coin chute. The world's first two-player game.

1934
- Simple electric solenoid kickers appeared on many games to add exciting effects to the game. Bally's Fleet and Genco's Spitfire are early examples. The kicker often took the form of a gun or cannon.
- In December 1934 the first small backglass appeared on Criss Cross, a tic-tac-toe game.

1935
- The first backboards. Initially they were only a few inches high and without lights, the backboard usually having the name of the game and operating instructions on it.
- George Molentin started working for Advertising Posters.
- Bally's Rockelite had a small backglass with illuminated scoring display.
- Harry Williams invented the first electric tilt indicator (initially called a stool pigeon) which cut the power to a game if it was manhandled. The device is still used today.
- Most pintables now had wooden legs fitted.

1936
- Mains transformers began to replace batteries on most new machines.
- Rockola introduced Totalite with small electric light bulbs scoring the total, a method used until 1960.

1937
- Bally introduced the first scoring bumper on its appropriately named Bumper. A coiled metal spring, approximately 1.5 inches in diameter, was suspended from a post, and when hit by a ball completed an electrical circuit so increasing the score. Previously, scoring was by balls dropping into holes.

1938

● The backbox had grown in size to near today's dimensions and the artwork was assuming a more important role in attracting players.

1939

● The first machine with an animated backglass appeared. Exhibit Supply Company's Contact game featured an aeroplane taking off from the flight deck of an aircraft carrier.

1941

● All pinball production ceased with relevant materials being used for the war effort.

1942

● Pinball declared illegal in New York on January 21st, 1942, and not rescinded until 1976.

1946

● Harry Williams set up in business as Williams Manufacturing. The first Williams' game was called Suspense.

1947

● The flipper was invented by Gottlieb engineer, Harry Mabs, and was first used on Humpty Dumpty in October 1947. Six flippers used.
● Williams introduced games with scores going into the millions. High-scoring targets and bumpers gave players a greater sense of psychological achievement.
● Keeney's Cover Girl had seven flippers.

1948

● The solenoid powered bumper was introduced by Bally and quickly adopted by all manufacturers. Gottlieb called them 'pop bumpers', Williams 'jet bumpers', Bally's 'thumper bumpers', and Genco 'power bumpers'.
● Genco's Triple Action was the first to use just two flippers at the bottom of the playfield, where they are still positioned today – a Steve Kordek innovation.

1951

● Gottlieb introduced the slingshot kicker, and Williams adopted it slightly later. The slingshot kicker gave the ball added impetus when it rebounded against stretched rubber rings usually mounted just above the flippers. The device has

become standard on virtually every pinball machine ever since.

1954

● Gottlieb's Super Jumbo was its first multi-player machine (for four people) and the first to use electric step-up reels for scoring.

1955

● Race the Clock was Williams' first multi-player machine (also for four people).

1956

● Bally brought out Balls-a-Poppin', the only pinball machine Bally made between 1950 and 1963 and its first multi-player (for two people). It was also the first multi-ball game, with up to six balls simultaneously in play.

1957

● Varnished wooden legs were gradually replaced by metal ones.
● The number match features at the end of the game was introduced by both Gottlieb and Williams.

1958

● Electrical step-up score reels appeared on single player machines for the first time on Williams Club-House. Within three years scores lit by bulbs, as used for many years, had been replaced by score reels.
● Williams Gusher (and Sea Wolf, 1959) had a disappearing jet bumper which lowered flush with the playfield.

1960

● The varnished natural wood rails on each side of the playfield glass were replaced by stainless steel, and those surrounding the backglass were removed.
● Alvin Gottlieb introduced the add-a-ball game. Gottlieb's Flipper was the first add-a-ball machine, introduced for locations where awarding a replay or free game for a high score was considered to be a prize and therefore illegal.
● Dancing Dolls was the last Gottlieb game to use bulb scoring.

1961

● George Molentin became art director of Advertising Posters.
● Spaceship was the last Williams game to use bulbs

in the backglass for scoring.

1962
- Steve Kordek devised the first single drop target, first used on Williams' Vagabond.

1963
- Williams' Beat-the-Clock was its first multi-ball game with two balls in play simultaneously.
- Gottlieb's Swing Along was the first to use the popular roto-target, while Gottlieb's Sweethearts was the last game to use gobble holes, so popular with manufacturers and hated by players during the 1950s.

1964
- The use of five separate balls lifted onto the playfield by a plunger was replaced by an automatic ball lift recirculating just one ball.
- The first mushroom bumper appeared on Bally's Monte Carlo, conceived by designer Ted Zale. Mushroom bumpers operated a switch under the playfield, and were extensively used by Bally in the 1960s and early 1970s.

1965
- Williams' Pot O'Gold was the first to use abstract art.
- Gottlieb's Bank-A-Ball was the first to use flipper return lanes whereby the ball would exit the playfield at the side and roll back down onto the flippers.

1966
- Zipper flippers which closed together preventing the ball leaving the playfield were introduced by Bally and first used on Bazaar in October 1966, but these flippers lost their popularity and were dropped after a few years.
- Bally introduced Six Sticks, a six-player game with a hockey theme.
- Roy Parker's last game, Gottlieb's Mayfair, was released in 1966 and Parker died shortly afterwards. Altogether he was responsible for the artwork for around 350 pinball machines.

1967
- Gottlieb's Super Score incorporated the score reels into the backflashes of two pinball machines shown in the backglass artwork.

1968
- Gottlieb's Paul Bunyan, like Humpty Dumpty, had six flippers.
- New larger 3 inch flippers first appeared on Williams' Hayburners II.

1969
- Williams introduced the up-post, a plastic cylinder which raises and lowers between the flippers, either preventing the loss of the ball when up or allowing it to exit if down. First seen on Williams' Cabaret.
- New larger size flippers were used on Bally's Ballyhoo which had two sets – one large, one small.
- The Who had a hit record with *Pinball Wizard*.

1970
- Gottlieb's Snow Derby introduced the end-of-ball bonus system in scoring, ever since a regular feature.
- Gottlieb's first game with the new larger flippers was Playball.
- Chicago Coin's Big Flipper had 5 inch flippers.

1971
- Gottlieb's 2001 was the first to use in-line banks of drop targets.

1972
- Pinball is legalised in Los Angeles.
- Williams' Spanish Eyes was the first to use DC electrical current for the playfield components to give added power.
- Bally's Fireball was the first to use a flat spinning disc on the playfield, called a whirlwind spinner. The idea was later used by Williams on Whirlwind which used three spinning discs.

1973
- Williams' Travel Time incorporated a working clock into the game.

1974
- Brian Protheroe had a minor hit with a record called *Pinball*.

1975
- Ken Russell's mystical rock-opera movie, *Tommy*, went on general release, starring Roger Daltrey as 'The deaf, dumb and blind kid who sure plays a mean pinball'. Also starring Ann-Margret, Oliver Reed, and Elton John.

- Italian manufacturer Zaccaria produces its first pintable, Lucky Fruit.

1976

- D Gottlieb & Co was sold to Columbia Pictures for $55 million.
- Bally produced a one-off giant pinball machine measuring 10 x 4 feet called Big Foot. It was made for a television show in which personalities competed in different sports.
- Elton John had a hit record with *Pinball Wizard* in the wake of *Tommy*.
- Pinball was legalised in New York and Chicago.

1977

- The electro-mechanical step-up units, score reels and relays, etc., were replaced by solid state microprocessors giving wider scope to the pinball designers.

1978

- Williams used a curved banana shaped flipper on Disco Fever.
- The first photographic backglass using the new four-coloured technique was Bally's Lost World. All previous games had been printed using the silk screen process.
- Letraset Ltd brought out a typeface called 'Pinball', designed by Alan Dempsey, in its dry lettering range.

1979

- Williams' Flash was the first game to use electronic sound effects. Gorgar was the first with speech.
- The electronics company Heathkit produced a self-assembly version of Bally's Fireball, priced at $600 in the USA.
- George Molentin retired from Ad Posters after 44 years.

1980

- Magna-save was introduced by Williams. A powerful electromagnet under the playfield operated by an extra button on the side of the cabinet enabled the player to 'grab' the ball and prevent it exiting down the out-lane. First used on Black Knight.
- Xenon was Bally's first talking pinball and featured the voice of Suzanne Ciani.

1981

- Artist David Christensen left Bally after 10 years, his last game almost bearing the same name as his first,

Fireball II.
- Bally's Centaur contained a reverberation unit which gave the voice a menacing echo as it roared out 'destroy centaur'.
- Black Hole was Gottlieb's first two-level game, but differed because the second level was below the main playfield and visible through a transparent panel set in the main area.

1982

- Gottlieb's Haunted House featured a three-level playfield.
- Stern Electronics brought out Orbiter I with a contoured three-dimensional playfield and revolving bumpers.
- Later that year Stern closed down its pinball division.

1983

- Harry Williams died. Williams was one of the pioneers of the pinball industry and invented many new ideas for the game, including the tilt mechanism. Roger Sharpe, author of *Pinball* and himself a pinball game designer called Williams 'the Thomas Edison of the pinball business'.

1985

- Bally-Wulff, Bally's new West German factory, produced Fireball Classic, the first pinball to be manufactured in West Germany. This was Bally's updated electronic version of the original 1972 Bally Fireball.

1986

- Williams' High Speed introduced automatic replay percentaging which automatically adjusted the replay score depending on the number of free games previously awarded.
- Gottlieb used the first photographic backglass with a real person on Raven.

1987

- A new major manufacturer started producing pinball machines, Data East, with its first game Lazer War.

1988

- Williams took over the manufacture of Bally pinball machines.

1989

- Data East fitted the first solid-state flippers to Robo-Cop.

INDEX